Adventures of a Semi-Reformed
Overachiever

# Adventures of a Semi-Reformed Overachiever

~

## LaNelle C. Stiles

Servant Publications
Ann Arbor, Michigan

© 1996 by LaNelle Stiles
All rights reserved.

Vine Books is an imprint of Servant Publications especially designed to serve evangelical Christians.

"God Hath Not Promised," by Annie Johnson Flint, is taken from the *Speaker's Treasury of 400 Quotable Poems*, Croft Pentz, ed. Copyrighted. Used by permission.

"Overheard in an Orchard," by Elizabeth Cheney, is taken from the *Donald T. Kaufman Compilation*, published by Fleming H. Revell in 1962. All rights reserved.

"Coping with Mr. Clean" first published in *Today's Christian Woman* magazine (May/June 1993).

Selected verses have been taken from the Living Bible (LB), the King James Version (KJV), and the New International Version (NIV) of the Bible. All rights reserved.

Published by Servant Publications
P.O. Box 8617
Ann Arbor, Michigan 48107

Cover design by Multnomah Graphics, Portland, Oregon

96 97 98 99 00 10 9 8 7 6 5 4 3 2 1

Printed in the United States of America
ISBN 0-89283-915-5

# dedication

To Ed

In spite of anything to the contrary
that might be suggested in this book,
when it comes to husbands
he's the greatest.

# contents

*Acknowledgments* / 9

Part One: Wave Good-bye to Wonder Woman / 11
  1. "Running out from under Myself" / 12
  2. The Battle of the Bulge / 20
  3. Who Says You're Not Getting Older? / 25
  4. Beauty and the Best / 29
  5. O Day of Rest and Gladness / 35
  6. Do It Now / 40

Part Two: Definitely Domestic / 45
  7. Going a Journey / 46
  8. Selective Hearing in the American Male / 50
  9. Why Pray When You Can Worry? / 54
  10. Coping with Mr. Clean / 59
  11. The Great Christmas Flush-out and other Holiday Memories / 64
  12. Y'all Come See Us / 72

Part Three: The Patience Principle / 79
  13. On the Road Again / 80
  14. Wrapped Up in Red Tape / 86
  15. What Do You Say to a Naked Fuchsia? / 91
  16. Winter Wonder-land / 95
  17. Four-footed Beasts and Creeping Things / 97
  18. "Ask the Animals, and They Will Teach You" / 106

Part Four: Chuckles and Complaints; Peeves and Pleasures / 113
  19. Dire Warnings and Signs of the Times / 114
  20. The Awful Truth (Or What People Won't Tell You) / 120

21. The Mauving of America / 126
22. Prayer and the Information Superhighway / 131
23. The Call of the Waves (Or How I Spent My Summer Vacation) / 135
24. Do You Smell What I Smell? / 140

Part Five: Insights and Outlooks / 145
25. Roses, Flat Tires, and Great Expectations / 146
26. Little Things Mean a Lot / 154
27. Friendship 101 (Or What I Didn't Learn in Kindergarten) / 158
28. Are You Serving More... and Enjoying It Less? / 164
29. Lurching along the Homeward Trail / 169

*Afterword / 175*

## acknowledgments

In the absence of experts, researchers, office assistants, and typists, I would like to thank the people who *really* made this book possible: my daughter Christi and my son Greg, my family, and all my friends. After all, they supplied me with the material. Their love, support, and encouragement have been priceless.

I would also like to express my appreciation to Beth Feia, senior editor at Servant Publications, for talking me into this project; and my editor, Cindy Maddox, of SilverFire Editorial Services, for helping me see it through to completion.

# part one

## Wave Goodbye to Wonder Woman
*Confessions of a Semi-Reformed Overachiever*

...she can laugh at the days to come. **Proverbs 31:25**

Wonder Woman may be alive and well and living somewhere in the world, but I don't know her and you probably don't either. Lots of us have tried wearing her hat—oops, headband—and all it gave us was a headache. But we do wear other hats—so many different ones that sometimes we don't have time to switch them and they stack up on our heads like the filling in a Dagwood sandwich. We've tried to have it all (somebody said we could) and do it all (nobody said we couldn't). And while we're doing it, we have to look good and stay slim and keep young. It's a tough job, but *nobody* really has to do it. At least that's what I've been telling myself: slow down. Chill out. Lighten up. And laugh a lot.

## one

## "Running out from under Myself"

The churchyard was full of kids on a summer Sunday evening. We were playing tag and chasing lightning bugs and generally undoing all the scrubbing and combing and pigtailing that had gone into getting us ready for church. I came flying pell-mell around the corner, running too fast for conditions, when I spotted my mother. I nearly lost my footing as I slid to a stop in the loose gravel.

"Whoops!" I cried. "I almost ran out from under myself!"

That's all it took. Mama laughed until she was gasping for breath, wiping away tears with her ever-present hankie. "Running out from under myself" was a concept that just happened to strike her funnybone. Obviously, it didn't take much to break Mama up. For months afterward she would recall that moment: "I almost ran out from under myself," she would say, and be off again in peals of laughter.

That was an earlier era, when life moseyed along at a more peaceful pace. I never saw my mother rushed, hurried, or stressed-out. Busy, yes. In those days of wringer washers and treadle sewing machines, she worked hard at home, in the churches my father pastored, as well as outside the home—not by choice, long before it was the fashionable thing to do. But she never seemed to be in danger of "running out from under herself." No wonder the idea amused her so.

Me? I haven't slowed down since 1962. "Like sands through an hourglass" may describe the days of some people's lives, but mine is more like eggshells through a disposal. They whirl around, crunch up, and disappear down the drain.

I called a woman on church business the other day and she

said, "I can give you a minute and a half." Then she proceeded to spend ten minutes telling me how busy she was. A friend of mine called a minister about something that was bothering her, only to be told, "Four minutes is all I can spare." I guess when Jesus said "give to him who asketh of thee," he wasn't talking about time.

The funny thing is that many of us have taken to wearing our busyness like some sort of Olympic medal. We are world-class "runners." Bragging rights used to come from kids on the honor roll, hubby's promotion, or maybe a new station wagon. Now we sit around at lunchtime and play "Can You Top This?" with our daily schedules.

"I can't make the meeting tonight," one woman says. "After work I have to take my Great Dane for her self-esteem training. My appointment with my personal trainer is at five, and Grandma will go into cardiac arrest if I don't get her to bingo by seven. It's the night for my brother's Male Bonding Seminar, and his wife is on a business trip, so I promised to babysit the kids. I love my nephews and I don't mind helping out, but they think because I'm not married with children I don't have anything to do. Anyway, then I'll have to run home and practice for a couple of hours. My harp lesson is tomorrow and I haven't touched it for a week. And I've been putting in extra time at karate class since we have a demonstration at the mall this weekend."

"Is that all?" her friend replies. "I have to pick up the baby at the sitter's and take her to Bobbing Babies for her swimming class. Reginald has ballet practice after he works out at the gym. Susie has to get to the airport for her flying lessons. Afterward, my husband will leave work and meet us at the drive-up window of the SFC (Sugar, Fat, and Cholesterol) Pigout Parlor. If we time it right, he can pass me the food and I can hand him the baby in about thirty seconds, providing of course that my car window doesn't stick on the way down. Then he heads for his Cajun cooking class, dropping the baby off at his mother's on the way so I can make it to my night class in neurosurgery. Later, he'll pick up the kids, the dog, and the baby so they can practice their Japanese language tapes in the car. All I have to do when I get home is iron his socks, whip up a seven-layer torte, scrub the grout between the bathroom tiles, and hit the sack."

When we're overprogrammed, overcommitted, and overworked, is it any wonder we're overtired, overwrought, and overweight?

Remember the old song, "Anything You Can Do I Can Do Better" from *Annie Get Your Gun?* Today it's more like "Anything You Can Do I Can Do More Of." I know "they" say, "If you want something done, find a busy person to do it," but "they" aren't always right. Common sense (that most uncommon quality) says that if you have too many things to do, pretty soon you won't be doing anything very well. And you won't be enjoying any of it.

Listen. I've been there. And it's not just jobs, home, and family that put the pressure on. Often it's the church. A few years ago I took time to count the church-related activities written on our calendar for one month—not everything that went on, just the ones we would be expected to attend. Twenty-seven.

It took me a long time to get my Sundays under control. I'm still working on the other days of the week.

A few years ago a best-selling book asked *Are You Running With Me, Jesus?* Personally, I doubt it. If the Lord didn't go running off to Bethany when Lazarus was sick, I don't think he would be inclined to rush around after us. Besides, aren't we the ones who are supposed to follow Christ—not vice versa?

Can you think of any time in the Bible when Jesus got in a hurry? When he rushed around in a panic? He was four days late, as far as Martha was concerned, in responding to the news of Lazarus' death. On his way to see the daughter of Jairus, he stopped and took time to speak to a woman who had crept close enough to touch the hem of his robe and be instantly healed of a long-standing illness. Jesus had time. Time for others. Time for himself, too.

Can't you just imagine how impatient the disciples must have become that day when they came back from buying lunch at the Samaritan VII-XI and found Jesus deep in conversation with someone who was clearly not prospective church board material. And a woman, at that! After so long in the hot sun, the Goliath Grape Gulps were approaching fermentation and the Herod's Halibut Hero sandwiches were emitting a distinctly fishy smell. And Jesus just sat there, talking. No hurry. After all, what did he have to do except proclaim the gospel of salvation, heal the lame, give sight to the blind, raise the dead, and carry out the eternal plan of Almighty God in redeeming a fallen world?

Now, what were all those important things I have to do?

Even after doing our very best to put our responsibilities in perspective, we are still, of necessity or by choice, busier than we ought to be. We feel overworked and underappreciated. We put Lady Perfection on one side of the scale and climb up on the other side. Then we weigh ourselves in the balance and come up wanting. So much for "having it all."

To make matters worse, along comes somebody waving the thirty-first chapter of Proverbs at us: "She gets up while it is still dark; she provides food for her family... she sets about her work vigorously... her lamp does not go out at night." Don't be intimidated. That woman ran a *household*. She was an *executive*. The Virtuous Woman of Proverbs 31 didn't try to do everything herself. She was a manager. She had servants and nursemaids and a houseful of relatives to share the responsibility. Like our grandmothers had. OK, maybe not the servants. But even the doddering great-aunts and spinster cousins and "between jobs" brothers-in-law—or whoever else rounded out the extended family—pitched in to get the work done.

In today's nuclear and single-parent families, we think we have to be a combination of Harriet Nelson, Cindy Crawford,

Florence Nightingale, Mother Goose, Betty Crocker, and Kathie Lee Gifford all rolled together. Get real.

To start with, get rid of that Wonder Woman costume. Send it to the flea market. Set a match to it. It probably doesn't meet safety standards anyway. Personally, I cut out bacon-and-egg breakfasts and Sunday pot roast dinners. Our arteries are better off and so are our dispositions. Find things that are expendable and expend them!

I've been working at this for a while, and even though I still get frazzled at times, I am learning to sort out the vital and necessary from the good and desirable. It's not easy. You can't just quit cold turkey. You can start by cutting back. Go into the bathroom. Lock the door. Look in the mirror. Place your tongue behind your upper teeth. Say n-n-n-n. Round your lips and say "o." Pretty soon you will be able to say "no." To the kids. To your family or neighbors or friends or whoever is using you up and sending you on a galactic guilt trip. You may need to turn down some of the jobs you are asked to do at church. There. I said it. I even put it in writing. (*I can't believe I said that!*) Saying "no" is not the Eighth Deadly Sin.

Here are some highly unscientific tests you can apply to see whether you are ready to join Overachievers Anonymous.

*Answer yes or no:*

- Do I find joy in all (some? any?) of the activities that engage my time?
- Do I actually find myself hoping a sneeze means a cold—a little one, of course—just bad enough to justify staying home?
- Is a canceled meeting or activity a disappointment or a relief?
- Am I willing to be snowbound just to get a break?

*Multiple choice:*

Am I doing this
   (a) for the Lord
   (b) for myself
   (c) for a loved one
   (d) because nobody else will do it
   (e) to impress someone
   (f) to please someone
   (g) because I feel guilty?

Choose all that apply.

*True-False:*

It (whatever it is) is worth the effort.

This is the key. When an activity is no longer fun or meaningful, when the rewards no longer outweigh the frustrations, it's time either to recharge your batteries or quit.

Now, what about all those kids' activities that demand our presence in three places at once and require the resources of an oil sheik to finance? If we say "no," will their psyches be destroyed, their emotional development stunted, and their lives ruined before they reach adolescence? If we refuse scuba diving lessons to a nine-year-old, we may risk never getting a Mother's Day card, being as lonely as the Maytag repairman on Christmases Yet to Come, and spending our golden years in a Home for the Filially Neglected. But we may ultimately be doing our kids a favor.

As a teacher I see it all the time—students who are far too involved in far too many activities, all of which are worthwhile. Many of these kids are being pushed by their parents and/or pressured by their peers. Are their activities something they really want for themselves? Or do they represent a delayed wish fulfillment for Mom or Dad? Are all the lessons, teams, and groups worth the strain on time, finances, emotions, and relationships? Will they have long-range benefits?

For years we frantically shuffled between ball games and horse shows and sometimes wondered why. Our son's college football scholarship helped answer that question. Although our daughter didn't ride for a few years, now, as a career woman, she is deeply involved in volunteer work with a Riding for the Handicapped program. These activities have proved their value.

On the other hand, we have our share of barely used trumpets and clarinets, like-new dancing shoes and gymnastic equipment, out-of-tune pianos, tennis rackets with rotting strings, and all kinds of other high-priced, much-coveted-and-longed-for paraphernalia gathering dust in attics and basements and closets. You probably do, too.

Maybe what we need in this country is another recovery group: Twelve Steps to Inertia. In case you have forgotten, inertia is the tendency of a body at rest to remain at rest. Oops, that won't work. You have to *be* at rest before you can remain that way.

Remember Mary and Martha? I am sure that Jesus appreciated all of Martha's scurrying around, but it was Mary's time, attention, and devotion that won his words of approval: "Mary has chosen the better part."

When I was a little girl, I memorized this clipping I found in my father's Bible:

> *Overheard in an Orchard*
>
> Said the sparrow to the robin,
> "I would really like to know
> Why these anxious human beings
> Rush about and hurry so."
>
> Said the robin to the sparrow,
> "Friend, I think that it must be
> That they have no Heavenly Father
> Such as cares for you and me."
>
> **Elizabeth Cheney**

Jesus told his disciples that they had more value than the sparrows. I suppose he also meant they had more sense. So if the birds—presumably equipped with bird brains—have got it figured out, why is it so hard for us to "be still and know that I am God"?

Fret not. Consider the lilies. Behold the birds. Freely translated, I think that simply means to slow down and get a grip. It may not be easy, but maybe it's time to try.

# two

## The Battle of the Bulge

In 1945 the Allies won the Battle of the Bulge. It was a glorious military victory. Since that time, however, the "battle of the bulge" has been fought on the home front, with millions facing their Retained Waterloo and taking Custard's Last Stand before going down in inglorious defeat before the onslaught of the Army of Fat Cells.

Maybe you never said it, but 'fess up now—didn't you ever *think*, "I can't believe she let herself go like that!" Well, I can believe it. Anyway, what's *let* got to do with it? I never heard a single pound ask *permission* to ride in your saddlebags. Who on earth would say, "I think I'll go ahead and gain some weight so I can buy myself a new wardrobe in Women's Wear"? Most of us oppose encroaching obesity with the determination of the French Resistance. We fight tooth and nail. Well, maybe the "tooth" part could use a little more effort.

Personally, I have developed a great interest in weight control. I can grab a Twinkie, crawl into the La-Z-Boy, turn on a workout tape, and read all the latest tips on how to slim down. The main bit of advice seems to be "change your eating habits." As if I hadn't. Except for the aforementioned Twinkie, of course.

Twenty years ago, a typical week's menus at our house would include pot roast with drippings-soaked vegetables, mashed potatoes with a puddle of brown gravy, fried okra, butter-slathered cornbread, candied sweet potatoes, fried chicken, meatloaf, and macaroni and cheese. Lunch was sandwiches with mayo and chips, breakfast wasn't breakfast without bacon, and I would have been embarrassed if I didn't have any homemade cake or pie to offer for dessert or a late-night snack.

Have an urge for an Oreo? Just check the cookie jar. M & M's? Malted milk balls? Sure. What were all those wedding-gift candy dishes for?

Our favorite snack was gigantic banana splits concocted with syrups brought home by our friends Glenn and Lill from the soda fountain in their drugstore. We didn't have the special dishes, but we didn't mind—we used soup bowls!

Homemade ice cream parties, taco parties, lasagna dinners—well, you get the picture. I can just hear you saying, "No wonder you were overweight!" Listen, I was a size 8.

Today I fry nothing, saute in water or broth, use Pam instead of Crisco, and eat cereal for breakfast (non-sugared, of course). I buy only lite, low-fat, no-fat, sodium-reduced, calcium-enriched products. I mean, nothing in my pantry is real! I substitute turkey for everything from ham to hamburger. I keep trying to fix up my husband Ed with Molly McButter and Mrs. Dash and keep him away from Mrs. Butterworth and Aunt Jemima. I've tried baked chips and baked nachos and baked crackers and they all taste like baked cardboard. Except the baked rice cakes, which taste like baked cardboard sprinkled with artificial sweetener. Speaking of sweeteners, I can't decide whether to go with the one that kills your brain cells or the one that causes cancer. Maybe all that broccoli and stuff will counteract it. I've eaten so much green stuff that my ears are growing long, my nose twitches, and I'm reasonably sure that was a whisker I tweezed away this morning.

Eat fruit, the experts say. We empty about two or three fruit baskets to one bottle of Kaopectate. By the way, why won't anybody ever eat that one last banana? It's always there, turning splotchy brown then blackening and shriveling up, pathetically alone and rejected. Do we fear the final banana? Is there some superstition I haven't heard of? My friend Mary Sue says that if she buys a dozen bananas, there's one left; if she buys five bananas, there's one left; and if she buys two bananas, there's still going to be one left. She throws hers away, but I am thriftier. I put mine in the freezer to save for banana bread. Of course, I haven't baked a loaf of banana bread in at least five years, but I still stash them away in the freezer. Waste not, want not, I always say.

Another popular how-to-lose-weight tip is to provide yourself with some incentives. Like a ceramic pig that sits inside the refrigerator and goes "oink, oink" when you open the door. Or pictures of yourself in skinnier days stuck on the fridge with little pig magnets. What about a vicious Pit Pig to stand guard in the pantry?

I tried buying clothes just a little too small. At first it was "this will be perfect if I lose five pounds," then it was ten pounds, and so on. Tucked away somewhere is a nice green bought-to-inspire-but-never-worn dress that I can't even get over my shoulders! I have others that can be worn quite comfortably—as long as I don't wish to sit down. Still others can be worn for sitting, but not for eating. One bite—if swallowed—would be side seam disaster. That's why I have decided that for me, the ultimate fashion statement is the elastic waistband. The only thing that feels even better is the elastic front panel. Well, it hasn't come to that—not yet.

I used to divide my clothes by the seasons: winter clothes, summer clothes. Now it's fat clothes and skinny clothes. And that's using the term "skinny" rather loosely. When the choice came down to dressing or breathing, I decided to hold off on any major purchases and just pick up a few inexpensive things to wear until I got the weight off. Now those "temporary" fat clothes are worn out and the skinny clothes are packed away, not to mention out of style. So what am I supposed to wear? My jeans have shrunk past the stage where I can lie flat on the bed and zip them up. I have one pair left that I can shoehorn myself into. Which reminds me—even my *feet* have gone up a size.

Let's face it. Gimmicks don't work and incentives don't work. That leaves diets, and everybody knows they don't work. Ed has one he swears by but never follows. Who would? It seems to be based on the concept of eating dried fruit and drinking lots of water. You don't need a degree in nutrition to imagine the ramifications of that one.

We have another popular three-day diet that consists of hot dogs, beets, and vanilla ice cream. I'd rather fast. The most sensible diet is the one involving the food pyramid and all kinds of "exchanges." I like that idea. I would gladly exchange anything on it for some KFC extra crispy, McDonald's fries, and a DQ hot fudge sundae.

"Lose Ten Pounds! The Twenty-Minute Solution!" The headlines screamed at me from the cover of a magazine I picked up in the beauty shop yesterday. I got pretty excited until I discovered that it had nothing to do with losing ten pounds in twenty minutes. The idea is to eat a small amount and wait twenty minutes until the "full" feeling kicks in. My problem is that the feeling kicks in much sooner than that. I'm hungry again in twenty minutes.

Now they're saying that the common-sense approach is the best one. Eat a balanced diet. I always thought a balanced diet meant not going to Pizza Hut more often than Wendy's. The secret, I was told, is drinking eight glasses of water a day. I do believe that is sixty-four ounces. We're talking a *half-gallon*. For someone who already has to schedule pit stops more carefully than Mario Andretti at the Indy 500, that's a bit much. I'd have to quit my job, avoid car trips of more than fifteen minutes, and stake out a claim to the quick-escape pew in the back of the church.

Another frequently offered tip for those of us who are not overweight but undertall is to dress to disguise figure flaws. This is never more important than when choosing a bathing suit. There are designs that will compensate for (a) small bust, (b) thick waist, (c) full hips, (d) heavy thighs. If, however, your problem happens to be (e) all of the above, you're out of luck. Stick with Omar the Tentmaker.

This brings us to the final suggestion. Have you seen those little plaques with a picture of a sheep that say, "Ewe's not fat; ewe's fluffy"? Cute, huh? Sheep may be fluffy, but people are flabby. And, as everyone knows, the only way to firm up and burn fat is exercise. This inevitably involves various means of locomotion other than the automobile, athletic activities requiring a certain measure of hand-eye coordination, contortion of the body into awkward, uncomfortable, and potentially lethal positions, painful shortness of breath, and perspiration. It doesn't take a rocket scientist to figure out why this is the most unpopular solution.

Just call me "Fluffy."

# three

## Who Says You're Not Getting Older?

The only thing worse than getting older is, of course, not getting older.

"Oh, to be a child again" may appeal to some people, but not to me. I would most certainly not want to be an adolescent. Not even a twentysomething. The thirties aren't bad, but the truth is you don't really start figuring out what it's all about until you pass the big 4-0.

It's too bad that just about the time you get your head together, your body starts to fall apart. All these years you've watched everybody else in your demographic group gain weight and lose height, develop frown lines and crow's feet, and sprout renegade hair in ears and other unlikely yet highly visible spots. You may have noticed the autumnal colors of advancing age: teeth turn yellow, hair goes gray, necks get red splotches, and hands develop brown spots. Still, some defense mechanism in your brain won't let you believe it will ever happen to you.

I used to roam around in the high school cafeteria, performing that specialized assignment for which I had eighteen years of education—cafeteria duty. I would try to picture my own elementary-school youngsters sitting at those tables, being initiated into various rituals of adolescent dining such as the shooting of peas through drinking straws and the popular but frowned-upon activity known as Jello sucking. I couldn't. My own kids old enough to be a part of that anxiety-ridden, hormone-driven crowd? Impossible. Actually, what I couldn't picture two decades ago was myself old enough to have kids in high school.

*Tempus fugit*, my algebra teacher Miss Rogers used to say. I never understood why she had to use Latin to tell us that time was flying, but when you're thirteen you're not going to believe it in any language. Summers were long and lazy, and one Christmas an eternity from the next.

But somewhere along the road from adolescence to adulthood, time picks up speed and propels you right over the hill. Once you are headed downhill, it gains momentum, until the years are practically tripping over each other. So I'm still sweeping up pine needles and it's Christmas again. If I think something happened last week, it was last month. If I think it was last month, it was last year. And if I think it was last year, it was 1983.

Have you ever inquired about an acquaintance's daughter's imminent high school graduation, only to discover she has completed college and med school? Or been traumatized by someone who inquires about your own family without protesting, "You can't be old enough to have grown children!" That's when you know *tempus* has really *fugited.*

Your body is more honest than your mind, and it speaks the truth while your mind is still in denial. First thing you know, you're coming up with lines like this:

"I've always worn this size. This brand must run on the small side."

"My arms are too short for me to read this menu."

"Some idiot moved first base. It was never that far from home plate before."

Just in case we happen not to notice the toll the years are taking, there's always someone handy to point it out. Kids, who are nothing if not candid, are particularly adept at this.

"Hey, Mom, your arms are getting flabby." Thank you, dear, for sharing that with everyone within earshot. How nice that you have stopped mumbling and learned to speak so loudly and clearly. Children are indeed a blessing from the Lord.

"You look just like my great-grandmother!" This was uttered by an angelic-looking little girl as we walked hand-in-hand from the chapel to the dining hall. Not *grandmother—greatgrandmother*! I must have looked as shocked as a not-yet-forty-year-old camp director could look under the circumstances. "Except," the child hastened to add, "you're much younger." Whew!

A student came into my room one morning with some money she owed the sophomore class. I assured her she was in the right place. "Oh, good," she replied. "They told me to see Mrs. Stiles, but I didn't know whether it was the young one or the old one."

Well, since the other Mrs. Stiles was in her first year of teaching, it wasn't hard to figure out which one I was. I was all of thirty-five!

Advancing age also requires that you make certain adaptations in your behavior. For example, I never wear shorts when we travel in the car. This is not because of the air conditioning. It's because I'm the navigator and I'm afraid I'll get us lost when I'm holding a map in my lap. You know all those little red and blue lines? They sort of all run together....

Growing older sometimes means a shrinking circle of friends. That may be true, but you also make a lot of new acquaintances like Dr. Scholl, Ben Gay, or perhaps even that well-known cowboy, Slim Fast. If you get busy and overdo, Charley Horse might drop in for a visit, and you can always count on Arthur Itis to stop by. Be prepared, though. He's a little on the wild side and likes to move from one joint to another.

The line between "middle age" and what is euphemistically called "maturity" is pretty blurry. Certain indicators are more reliable than the calendar when it comes to letting you know when it's time to sign up with AARP and start asking waiters for the Senior Citizen's menu:

When you walk with your head held high because it's the only way you can see the curb in your new bifocals.

When your rocking chair has to be jump-started.

When dialing long distance leaves you out of breath.

When you read the obituaries every morning to see whether your name is there.

When the only reason you dine by candlelight is to save on the electric bill.

When you know all the answers but have forgotten the questions.

When your knees buckle more easily than your belt.

Back in the late Medieval Period when I was in college, a fellow student got up in our Sunday school class to introduce the guest singers, members of the church who had been together for quite a few years. Not knowing the name of their group, he presented them simply as the "Old Men's Quartet."

Of course that wouldn't happen today. We are much too sensitive to political, cultural, and semantic correctness. Any such group today would no doubt be called something with "golden" in it. But let's face it: "golden" is just one letter away from "olden."

Old or young, people are never satisfied with their age. Children can't wait to be teenagers. Teens can't wait to be adults. Adults want to be young again. Why can't we just enjoy all the good things about each season of life—the promise of youth and the fulfillment of maturity? Just the way God planned it.

"I have created you and cared for you since you were born. I will be your God through all your lifetime.... I made you and I will care for you" (Is 46:3-4 LB). To which I would add the plea of David: "Now also when I am old and gray-headed, O God, forsake me not" (Ps 71:18 KJV).

Amen and amen!

# four

## Beauty and the Best

I heard on TV the other day that the average woman uses twenty-six products—I'm talking health and beauty aids, not food items and certainly not cleaning supplies—before she leaves the house every morning. Think of it! It takes more than two dozen creams, lotions, sprays, gels, roll-ons, lather-ups, and rinse-outs to get me presentable enough to face the world. Or rather, to have the world face me without being scared to death or at least seriously offended.

Ah, the price of being glamorous. Let's not go that far—beautiful. No, cross that out. Good-looking? Attractive? Well, let's settle for adequate. We pay a high price, if anybody could take time out from all that body tending to calculate it. And it's not just the cost of all those products. They don't come cheap in spite of the ready availability of seaweed, mud, lanolin (a.k.a. sheep fat), vitamin E, and other hypoallergenic and semi-miraculous concealers of truth. You have to consider the time you spend applying and blending and blotting and spraying and rubbing in and rinsing out, not to mention the wear and tear on your nerves when you sneeze three time while your mascara's still wet. Other family members sometimes have to pay a price, too. Especially when Mom's running late on a bad hair day.

Some busy women who can't be bothered with all the time and trouble of applying makeup every day can now enjoy the effect without all the effort. All it takes is a visit to their friendly neighborhood tattooist to have color permanently applied. Toss out your blush brush, your lipstick, your eyeliner pencil. It can all be done with a needle!

Amazing, isn't it—or perhaps appalling is a better word—the extremes to which women will go in the effort to improve their appearance? Or at least make themselves think they look better. One of the recent fads is lip augmentation—making your lips fuller than heredity intended, à la Julia Roberts and that ever-popular role model, Madonna. I always thought a fat lip was something you tried to avoid by not sassing your parents and staying out of bad neighborhoods.

There appears to be no end to the anatomical areas that can be enhanced by the marriage of medicine and technology. If you have never read *Coma* or seen the movie and don't mind being anesthetized and sliced open with sharp knives, you can have implants almost anywhere in your body: breast, chin, nose, fanny (although why anyone would want this is beyond my personal powers of comprehension)—you name it. Too bad there isn't a common sense implant also available. Oh well, cosmetic plastic surgeons have to send their kids to college, too.

Augmentation is hardly our primary concern, however. Mother Nature has already augmented us right out of the Junior Department to the sections where Real Women shop and the tags read "full cut." Not to worry. Dr. Hoover stands ready with his liposuction machine to vacuum away those saddlebags, suck out that tummy bulge, and hand you a one-way ticket out of Cellulite City. For a while.

By the way, did you ever wonder what they *do* with all that excess adipose tissue once it's removed? Transplant it into desperate patients on the thin-lipped waiting list? Move it from your fanny to your face? (It sort of gives the phrase "cheek to cheek" a whole new meaning, doesn't it?) You can't just dump the stuff—look what happened to Exxon. Maybe there could be commercial uses. Whale blubber was a big money-maker a century ago, you know.

Mirror, mirror... oh, who cares? Why are we so obsessed with how we look? It would be easy to point yet another accusing finger at television, which has certainly helped to promote this whole beauty-is-all phenomenon, but that would be not only unfair but inaccurate. This thing didn't just start with "I'm worth it" commercials. Nor did it begin with Halo-glorified hair back in the days of radio or with those full-page magazine spreads asking "Which twin has the Toni?" From the first time a woman caught a glimpse of her own reflection and said, "My hair looks awful!" human beings—especially but not by any means exclusively those of the female persuasion—have been universally dissatisfied with their appearance. Throughout the centuries, therefore, they have painted and padded, plucked and plaited, stretched and flattened, trained and tortured, and alternately concealed and displayed various parts of their anatomy to conform to some artificial standard of beauty as it was perceived by their society and the age in which they lived.

The Chinook Indians, for example, greatly admired elongated skulls, so their babies were bound to boards in order to produce a head of admirable proportions. The ancient Chinese crippled little girls by binding their feet to achieve a desirable characteristic. The Burmese put rings around their children's necks as they grew, creating a long, slender neck so weak it would break if unsupported. We've all seen Scarlett O'Hara hanging on to the bedpost while Mammy tightened her stays down to the mandatory eighteen inches, but in sixteen-century Europe, the ideal was thirteen inches. This wasp-waisted effect was no doubt encouraged by men who made fortunes in corsets, iron stays, whalebone, and, more recently, plastic, not to mention the manufacture and sale of the smelling salts necessary to revive the poor ladies who were constantly passing out for lack of air. "Fainting couches" were standard parlor furniture for Victorian homes. No wonder.

Why do we keep playing the game? Especially when they keep changing the rules. In 1924 Miss America was 5'4", 137 pounds. Today she has to be 5'10" and 110.

At the turn of the century, the ideal "Ziegfeld Girl" was 36-26-38. Big hips, big hair! Then along came the scandalous Twenties, when girls showed their knees but bound anything that curved in order to achieve a figure that was as flat and boyish as possible.

Through it all, the center of attention has been the hair. No torture is too painful, no expense too great, no time too valuable when it comes to the woman's crowning glory. And she has crowned it with some pretty glorious, not to mention outlandish, toppings. During the time of Charles V of France, palace doors had to be made higher and wider to accommodate the ladies' headdresses, which were a foot high and up to four feet wide. This fashion swept the continent, and ministers had a heyday exhorting against these feminine excesses, warning women that these ornaments of pride would bring them to destruction, except they repent.

The fashionable eighteenth-century woman endured the weight of hairstyles that towered up to three feet high and threatened everyone's safety as flowers and feathers brushed dangerously near burning candelabra. These styles were generously padded and filled with all manner of astonishing adornments, including ships in full sail, zoos and aviaries filled with glass animals and birds, the solar system (revolving!), and, in one creative woman's case, a miniature version of her departed husband's tombstone. Another grieving widow wore a model of a hearse drawn by six white horses.

It was at this point in history, I believe, that long-handled head scratchers were invented. They eventually disappeared from the scene, only to reappear when the 1960s "beehives" became the rage. I know from personal experience that they were in demand. I used to get my hair done once a week, wrap my updo in toilet paper, put on a huge net cap, and sleep with a pillow under my neck. (Maybe that's one reason my chiropractor enjoys so much of my company today.) If you recall, the "flip" was also a popular style at this time. My students used to get up at 5 A.M. so they could tease and lacquer their hair into an immobile S-shape and get to school by eight.

But this is the nineties, right? We're liberated, right? Secure in our femininity, right?

I was getting a cut in the beauty shop a few weeks ago when I heard cries of pain coming from the back room. Not screams; it was more like little yelps. At first I thought someone had overstayed their time in the tanning bed (my son calls it a "cancer clam"), but I was quickly reassured. It was only a routine eyebrow pluck.

If you've ever been highlighted, I'm sure you will agree with my theory that the frosting cap is a modification of some instrument of torture used in the Spanish Inquisition. Why do I sit quietly and allow someone to gouge my scalp repeatedly with a sharp instrument? Permanents have come a long way from those snaky Medusa-like machine jobs, but if your hairdresser rinses and squeezes those rigid little curlers painlessly, the job probably isn't being done properly. Then, when it's all over, you have to pay for the privilege of being tortured.

I know a lot of women who sit patiently for the application of acrylic nails. Did you know those things are flammable? Be careful when you light the candles on the dining room table, or you'll be qualified to perform an authentic impromptu rendition of "This Little Light of Mine."

I think it's safe to say that we can smile at the follies of the past, being far too sensible in these modern, enlightened times to follow the whims of fashion. Unless, of course, we ever wore crinoline petticoats, pointed-toe shoes, stiletto heels, teased hair, tent dresses (pregnancy excluded), granny glasses/dresses, and skirts in which you cannot sit, walk, or bend over. Can you believe those potentially lethal platform-soled shoes are back? Soon we'll hear of a lawsuit against a manufacturer because some customer fell off her shoes. Remember when "Your mother wears combat boots" was an insult? Now lovely young girls wear them with delicate chiffon dresses. Whalebone corsets may be out of style, but I just counted twelve pages of "foundation garments" (a.k.a. "girdles") in the JCPenney catalog.

What masochistic instinct drives us to all this self-inflicted discomfort? Do we do it for men? Other women? Ourselves? Not even our hairdresser knows for sure.

There is Someone who does know, a whole lot better than we

know ourselves. I sometimes wonder what the Lord thinks of all our crazy efforts to improve upon what we were born with. I think his attitude must be a mixture of amusement and compassion, maybe with a dash of annoyance that we spend so much time and energy on something so ultimately unimportant in his sovereign plan.

But God does understand. The Lord knows our insecurities, our needs, our fears. Everybody wants to measure up, to fit in, to meet with approval. That's fine, as long as we don't lose sight of what is truly worthy of admiration: inner beauty that is the reflection of a virtuous life.

I have a feeling that if we were to line up photographs of celebrated, drop-dead gorgeous faces—Greta Garbo, Elizabeth Taylor, Marilyn Monroe, Grace Kelly, Sophia Loren, Cindy Crawford—and then put a picture of Mother Teresa right in the middle of the batch, her face would be the one that grabbed your attention. And your heart.

Still, I can't help agreeing with St. Paul who was, research seems to indicate, no beauty himself: "How weary we grow of our present bodies. That is why we look forward eagerly to the day when we shall have heavenly bodies...." (2 Cor 5:2 LB).

Since the "present body" that has been given unto me is already a sort of biblical one—"pressed down, shaken together, and running over," I wonder if it's OK to "covet earnestly" one that is tall and thin. And, if it's not asking too much, blonde.

# five

## O Day of Rest and Gladness

Sometimes I like to thumb through old hymnbooks just to see what the old-timers sang that we have forgotten about. Many of the hymns are timeless, as much loved today as a century ago: "Amazing Grace," "How Firm a Foundation." Some of the more interesting and unusual songs are rarely heard. We tend to avoid those with colorful imagery like "Life's Railway to Heaven," "Turn Your Radio On," or "The Royal Telephone." We're not that big on extended metaphors, I guess, even when they offer us reassurance that the phone line to heaven is never busy. And you never—O blessed thought—*never* get an answering machine. Can't you just hear it: "If your request is spiritual, press 1; if it is physical, press 2; financial, press 3..."

For some reason, heaven isn't nearly as popular a theme as it used to be. And when we do sing about heaven, it's not likely to be called "Beulah Land." Other obscure songs with intriguing titles have totally disappeared from the gospel music scene. Have you ever heard "No Parking Here" or "Elbow Room"? I didn't think so.

Some hymns have a way of always reappearing in newer editions but rarely—if ever—being sung. "O Day of Rest and Gladness" is a good example. I presume the day in question is Sunday. If so, either our forefathers knew something we don't know, or times have really changed.

Sunday, according to the words of this hymn, is the best day of the week because it is an "emblem of eternal rest." Anybody today who thinks Sunday is a day of rest should take a drive down to the mall. "O Day of Haste and Shopping" would be a lot more fitting. Or maybe "O Day of Laundry and Housework," or for the kids, "O Day of Last-Minute Homework."

"O Day of Golf and Fishing" might work for some. People who

pursue these activities assure me that they are relaxing. Maybe... after the sunburn, backaches, muscle strain, and bad tempers have been treated. Organized sports for kids with names preceded by "little," "midget," and "pee-wee" have commandeered Sunday as yet another day to frazzle your nerves, exhaust your body, and empty your pocketbook. Especially at the end of the season. Is it wrong to pray your team *won't* make the playoffs?

Sunday has become just another day for millions of workers, as "blue laws" have crumbled and more places of business are competing for the Sunday shopper's dollar. It has never been a day of rest for doctors and nurses, pharmacists and ambulance drivers, policemen and firemen, not to mention gas station attendants—but there was a time when the pace was considerably slower than during the rest of the week.

So much for a day of rest. But what about gladness? I don't think it's exactly what the hymnwriter had in mind, but people who don't have to go to work are glad. Church goers are glad when the sermon is over and they can quiet their growling stomachs. Fans are glad when their NFL team is playing on TV. I'm glad when "Murder, She Wrote" isn't a rerun.

What would our Puritan forefathers think? They saw Sunday as a day of rest, although not necessarily one of gladness. At least not the kind that could be noticed. Except for walking through the snow/heat to a freezing/stifling church and staying awake through a three-hour sermon, you could be fined for doing almost anything on Sunday. This included desecrating the day by laughing. Or by any other unnecessary and "frivolous" behavior.

For our parents and grandparents, Sunday was a day of rest—if you were a man. The men came home from church and sat on the porch until dinner was on the table. Afterwards they dozed in their rocking chairs while the women cleaned up, a process which took the biggest part of the afternoon. OK, in the winter the menfolk would have to feed the animals, or at least see to it that the kids did. Still, life did shift into a lower gear as nonessential chores were temporarily laid aside.

Today, almost anything goes on a Sunday. But when I was growing up, certain games and activities were verboten on the Sabbath, although we were allowed to read or listen to the radio, and later, watch television. In the early television era, those church folk who allowed this new instrument of the devil into their homes claimed they didn't watch on Sunday, except of course Billy Graham after church on Sunday night. I remember going to visit a family who had TV long before we did. Supposedly they were going to turn it on just for "The Hour of Decision." But I couldn't help wondering why that little white dot in the center of the screen was still fading away when we walked into the living room. Could Ed Sullivan have been Billy Graham's warm-up act?

I sometimes read fashion magazines at the beauty shop—it keeps my mind off the pain. One article which caught my eye was giving advice on how to get through the "worst day of the week"—Sunday of course. The author suggested a number of activities, none of which was remotely religious in nature and certainly did not involve public or private worship, and then concluded by saying that since Sunday was such a miserable day you had a perfect right to go ahead and feel lousy. I took umbrage. (I do that occasionally.) How dare she say such things! Upon reflection, however, I got honest enough to admit to myself that there had been many times I—the Cheerful Church Lady—dreaded to see Sunday come.

Why? First Day overload.

Here is what my typical Sunday morning used to be like: Get up, cook breakfast, start dinner, clean kitchen, make beds, get kids ready, dress. Nothing that can't be handled in an hour and a half, assuming nothing is ripped, broken, wrinkled, or missing. Assuming no one throws up or falls down. Assuming that the cattle or horses don't get out, which they seemed to do on Sundays with religious regularity. Off to church. Practice with soloist, teach Sunday school, play organ, lead choir, run downstairs and teach lesson in children's church, and, with expert timing, make it back to the sanctuary, hitting the organ bench like a baseball player sliding into home plate in a forced play, just in time to play "Jesus, I Come" for the closing hymn. We had a custodian who was as loyal to Pledge as he was to the church, and if I didn't grab hold, I would slide in on one side of the bench and right off on the other!

At home in the afternoon, it was time to cook dinner, clean up, practice music for evening service, get ready for whatever meetings and/or rehearsals preceded or followed the service, and hope to get home before ten o'clock. I'm much older now. And smarter. Just *thinking* about it, I have to take a pill and lie down.

I will admit to being as schizophrenic as the next Christian about how to keep Sunday the holy day it was intended to be. My "OK's" and "Not OK's" would no doubt amuse some and offend others. I probably wouldn't approve of yours, either. The New Testament Pharisees had 613 provisions of the Law that they tried to observe every day. We could take a survey and come up with more than that, I'm sure. They argued constantly about things like how many times you could tie your sandals on the Sabbath and how far you could carry your chair to get from the sun into the shade and if you dragged it in the dirt, was that plowing?

I'm not sure whether it's religious conviction or plain old nostalgia that makes me long for lazy Sunday afternoons when the streets were quiet and traffic was light. When the whole community slowed down and put its collective feet up for a few hours. When there was time for church and family and visiting friends and sitting on a squeaky porch swing or sauntering through the park (how long since you sauntered anywhere?) or "Cruisin' Down the River on a Sunday Afternoon." You didn't have to be religious to enjoy a Sunday break in the routine. Even if you were, it was more than a pause for spiritual refreshment—it was a time to visit friends, eat fried chicken and watermelon when there was "dinner on the grounds," and recharge your batteries for another week.

But those days are gone, and we can't do much about it. Where are you going to carry picket signs that say, "Give Us Back Our Sundays"? Nowhere. Considering the commercial ramifications, it's unlikely we will ever go back to those earlier, simpler days. But surely we can find some way to make Sunday special, to keep it different. To set it apart—as much as possible—from the secular.

There is something unnatural about the frenetic pace that keeps us going seven days a week, like a Las Vegas casino where there are no windows, the light is always artificial, and you can easily lose track of day and night. Nature operates in cycles, and six days of labor and one of rest is a part of that cyclical pattern established by God in creation.

If God thought it was a good idea to rest on the seventh day, maybe we should try it, too. And behold, it is *good.*

# six

## Do It Now

I've been thinking about procrastinating, but I've decided to put it off for a while.

Actually, I've been thinking about this for so long I've developed a philosophy which can be squeezed into a single maxim: Never do today what you can put off until tomorrow.

"Mañana is good enough for me" is a line stuck in my memory bank from some scratchy old Decca 78s we used to play on our faithful Motorola. If it sounds like your theme song, too, you're in excellent company. There are so many confirmed procrastinators out there that I've been considering organizing a support group—a sort of Procrastinators Anonymous. I just haven't gotten around to doing it yet. On the other hand, what's the point? Coming up with Twelve Steps would be easy, but why bother? Nobody who qualified for membership would be likely to make it past the first one. When we do finally get around to organizing, we'll start our meetings with the team cheer: "Two, four, six, eight, everyone procrastinate!"

"Are you feeling better now?" a friend asked me the other day on the phone. "I bought you a card, but I never got it in the mail." I was able to report that I had fully recovered from my bout with pneumonia—two months earlier. All summer I kept running into people who said, "I've been thinking about you. I'm sorry I never got a card in the mail. I meant to, but..."

I couldn't fault any of these well-meaning friends. I'm an expert at putting off buying and/or mailing get-well cards until the person is either fully recovered or dead. I'll buy a sympathy card and let it lie around until the deceased has been so long departed that I'm embarrassed to mail it. You always think you can use it another time, right? But when the time comes, you can't find it or it's totally inappropriate. No smug and superior smiles, now, please. How many "In Deepest Sympathy" cards do you have slowly yellowing in a drawer somewhere?

I think the person who invented the belated birthday card should be nominated for the Pulitzer Prize in Literature. If there were no belated birthday cards, my friends and family wouldn't get any birthday cards. Of course I know when their birthdays are. They come on the same day every year. I don't exactly forget them. I just don't remember at the right time. I think about it too early and then put it off until it's too late!

I'll never forget my sense of social indignation the first time I ever received one of those little engraved R.S.V.P. cards in a wedding invitation. "Where did this thing come from?" I wailed. Writing "2" on the line by "Number of Persons" didn't seem so bad, but what if I can't attend? Just put down "0"? That struck me like saying, "I'll tell you how many are coming. Zero, that's how many." Whatever happened to "Mrs. Farquhar regrets she will be unable...."? Of course, I know what happened to "Respond, if you please." Folks weren't pleased to respond and were putting off writing those accept/regret notes for so long that nobody knew how many little nylon net sacks of rice to make, let alone what to tell the caterer.

Correspondence notwithstanding, a nice healthy pile of clothes to be mended is the true procrastinator's dream. Mending can so easily be tucked away out of sight and out of mind. Indefinitely, even infinitely. My kids used to grow out of jeans waiting for a patch on the knee. My husband has to stand around in white shirt, tie, and underwear while I sew up a pants pocket. I do occasionally get around to sewing on buttons—but only when the garment is already being worn and the wearer is about to go out the door.

Sewing? I've had fabric for sofa pillows in my "gotta do"

basket at least five years. Two months ago I finally cut it to size. Unless the couch upholstery falls into shreds in the meantime, I'm going to finish those pillows just as soon as I get around to it. While I'm at it, maybe I'll hem those bell-bottoms. They'll be right in style!

I was going to call the piano tuner to come during the Christmas holidays last year when I was home from school, but I didn't get around to it. So I decided to wait until summer. Another school year is now well underway, and the piano still sounds like it belongs in a honky tonk café. Oh, well, it's only four months until another Christmas vacation.

For the past six months, the set of Calphalon cookware I had craved has been sitting inconveniently on the dryer in the laundry room, collecting lint and waiting for a permanent home in a yet-to-be-cleaned-out kitchen cupboard. I felt pretty badly about this situation until I was reading about the "odd couple" marriage of Mary Matalin, chief campaigner for George Bush, and James Carville, mastermind of the Clinton campaign. The only thing Mary really complained about in their opposites-attract relationship was the way James rattled pots and pans in the kitchen. It seems he has no place to keep his Calphalon cookware!

My son Greg is a Procrastinator *summa cum laude*. Since his father is a do-it-right-now kind of person, I can't imagine where he got the tendency. It must have been in the gene pool somewhere. Dad is, unfortunately, an enabler, since the child learned early that if he didn't refuse a request but simply and quietly postponed doing it, he would find that some impatient Type-A person had beat him to the job. His explanation was irrefutable: "I was *going* to do it!"

I blame my own tendency to put off certain tasks on my "phonophobia." I hate to use the telephone and always delay as long as possible any calls I can't get someone else to make for me. The calls I am most prone to avoid are to two of the nicest people I know: my dentist and my hairdresser. The procedures performed by the latter are only slightly less unpleasant than those of the former.

Here is a list of other things I can put off without so much as the flicker of an eyelash:

>going to the grocery store
>seeing my gynecologist
>exercising
>unloading the dishwasher
>ironing
>grading term papers
>picking beans
>going to bed
>getting up
>watering the plants
>parting with old magazines
>starting a diet
>defrosting the freezer
>planning a garage sale
>matching and folding socks

All of these omissions, if indulged in, will as a matter of course produce consequences, some more serious than others.

Last March the daffodils in the front yard bloomed splendidly. Big yellow stars perched atop rich green stalky leaves. Dozens of fat buds were ready to burst open in the rare, early fine weather. The temperature was in the 60s as I walked barefoot to the mailbox.

"Should I cover the flowers?" I wondered. The weatherman was predicting an overnight change, but it was easy on this warm afternoon to conclude that he didn't know what he was talking about.

Maybe later, I decided.

The next morning the temperature was in the teens and my daffodils were lying limp and blackened against a six-inch layer of snow.

"I'll do it later." How many kind and thoughtful gestures—a

call, a visit, a letter, a card, a compliment—had I neglected in the same way, with much more significant consequences? A lovely elderly lady in my church was a great comfort to me during a difficult time. I didn't really know her well, and we spoke only occasionally, but I'll never forget how her gentleness and kindness encouraged me. But I never told her. She's in her nineties now and doesn't always recognize people. Why didn't I take the time to tell her how I felt? It probably doesn't matter to her any more. But it does to me.

"Now is always best time!" says the King of Siam to schoolmistress Anna in *The King and I*. To which Scarlett O'Hara would have replied, "Tomorrow is another day." And they would both be right. Every day that God allows us is a new opportunity to put into practice St. Paul's admonition: "As we have opportunity, let us do good to all people...." (Gal 6:10 NIV)

Fortunately for the procrastinator, this is an opportunity that knocks more than once.

# part two

## Definitely Domestic

*May she who gives birth rejoice!* **Proverbs 23:25**

"Family values" is the catch-phrase of the 90s. While the politicians and the press are out there trying to figure out what a family is, you and I are busy trying to figure out how to get along with the one we have, whatever its immediate shape may be. St. Paul, bachelor though he was, shows a remarkable understanding of what family relationships are all about. "A profound mystery," he called it, to which we can all say a hearty "amen." Who isn't amazed when a couple celebrates forty or fifty or even sixty years of togetherness? People say it's often children who hold a marriage together. I'm inclined to agree. My husband and I always said that whoever walked out had to take the kids. We've been together for over thirty years.

Whatever your family situation may be, these little reflections on domestic life will strike a familiar chord with anybody who has any relatives at all.

## seven

## Going a Journey

"One of the pleasantest things in the world is going a journey." These words were written in 1822 by William Hazlitt, English essayist and without a doubt the last male in history to express such sentiments. But then Hazlitt was traveling on foot—by himself.

Strolling along the English byways and communing with nature is one thing. Put Hazlitt in a station wagon with four kids and a St. Bernard, dodging orange barrels, keeping an eye on the eighteen-wheeler in his rear-view mirror, and hoping it stays out of the suitcases and surfboards in the cargo space. Let him referee back-seat quarrels while driving seventy-five down an isolated interstate with no rest areas. Then see if the superlative form of "pleasant" is his adjective of choice.

We don't go on journeys today; we take vacations. The key word is *take*. Men see it as a challenge. You have to get that travel time by the throat, wrestle it to the ground, show it who's boss.

Don't get me wrong. Our family has terrific vacations. If you don't believe me, just drop by some evening. I'll lock the doors and crank up the slide carousel and the old Super 8 movie projector and take you from Disneyland to Disney World, from Hershey Park to Six Flags, from Yellowstone to Niagara Falls, from the vistas of the Grand Canyon to the beaches of the Grand Strand. The problem is not *being* on vacation. The problem is *going* on vacation.

"Are we there yet? Are we there yet?" You probably think the kids keep up this chant just to irritate you. Wrong. Kids are smart. They know that when a man is at the wheel, vacation doesn't start until you GET THERE. It's a Y-chromosome thing.

Most men, regardless of personal philosophy, become pragmatists when Going on Vacation—which simply means that the end (Being There) justifies the means (Getting There). Women, on the other hand, have the idea that you shouldn't have to wait five hundred miles to ask "Are we having fun yet?"

When a woman arrives at the home of a friend or relative in a distant city, does she boast of how many minutes she shaved off her personal best, driveway to driveway?

Like it *mattered*.

What is this testosterone-induced compulsion that turns a pleasure trip into a non-stop highway endurance marathon? I have had plenty of time to ponder this question as we whizzed past cornfields and cotton fields, tourist traps and scenic overlooks, restaurants and rest stops. Couldn't we, just once, on impulse, SEE ROCK CITY?

Once, in a cool-headed moment, I decided that anything that took so much time, energy, and money deserved to be discussed in a calm, rational manner. Why, I wanted to know, was stopping from time to time such a problem? Just help me understand. What difference did a few minutes here and there make? And I got a calm, rational answer. When we stop, I was told, all that traffic we had passed on the road would *pass us!*

Stunned by the simplicity of the reply, I found myself with nary a reasoned rebuttal or snappy comeback. How do you argue with that kind of logic? Or deal with the Richard Petty syndrome? I had never realized that every pair of taillights blinked a challenge: Bring it on! Pass me if you can!

Maybe I'm being unreasonable. After all, there is biblical support for such an attitude: "... and the driving is like the driving of Jehu the son of Nimshi; for he driveth furiously" (2 Kgs 9:20 KJV). Sometimes I *rideth* furiously, too.

Given the limitations of the human body and the internal combustion engine, however, there are some occasions where a stop is absolutely necessary. When such an undesirable situation arises, certain rules are in effect:

*A. General:*
  1. Can't stop in or near cities. Too much traffic.
  2. Can't stop on the open road. Making good time.
*B. Gas Stations:*
  1. Must be on right side of highway, easy access.
  2. Must have no other cars in evidence.
*C. Restaurants:*
  1. Must be certified "fast food."
  2. Must be in sight of exit (the restaurant—not just the sign.)
  3. No cars in the drive-through lane.
  Note: If stops at B and C coincide, the establishments must be adjacent.
*D. Motels:*
  1. Can't stop early. A waste of good driving time.
  2. Can't stop late. No point in spending money for just a few hours' sleep.

Even with all the rules in place, it's not that simple. When the fine and rare moment comes when everyone is starving and the Golden Arches are in sight, where is Jehu? Driving furiously in the inside lane of a four-lane highway. "Oh," he says, "was that the exit?"

That big "Rest Area One Mile" sign is, at times, a welcome sight to weary and uncomfortable travelers. Unfortunately, this is also the exact moment when the driver decides to pass three tractor trailers, which effectively blocks any attempt to exit. No problem. There's another sign: Next Rest Area 47 Miles.

All of which makes this experience more delicious: We were coming home from the beach. Lying down in the back seat, I overhead this conversation:

"Let's stop at this next rest area."

"But we just stopped an hour ago!"

Sound familiar? Sure. But this time it was Dad (in the passenger seat) wanting to stop, and Number One Son (in the driver's seat) raising the protest!

I love it. Sometimes justice does prevail, even when it's poetic justice. It's great to live long enough to see some of the chickens come home to roost.

Hey, nobody said it would be easy. But maybe the wedding vows should include "on vacation and at home" along with "in sickness and in health." If your marriage survives Going On Vacation, you are then ready for reeealy big challenges: Putting Up The Christmas Tree and Hanging Wallpaper.

The old-timers used to sing "When I Take My Vacation in Heaven." Too bad that song isn't around any more, even though I always thought heaven was a permanent residence rather than a vacation spot. Theology aside, what could have a more powerful appeal for men? Whenever the time comes to make that final trip, they know they are going to love it. After all, they're going to get there in the twinkling of an eye!

# eight

## Selective Hearing in the American Male

"Why can't a woman be more like a man?" asks Professor Henry Higgins in *My Fair Lady*. Consciousness-raising has made this male chauvinist question as outmoded as Scarlett O'Hara's corset. Today the question has been reversed. Why, we want to know, can't men be more like women: more sensitive, more nurturing, more communicative?

Read the women's magazines. "He doesn't *listen* to me!" is the most frequent cry of modern women about the men in their lives.

Relax. Stop complaining. Maybe we're being too hard on the fellows. Recent medical studies have turned up some evidence that, in fact, men don't hear as well as women. And here we are, blaming the poor guys for something they can't help! How could we ever have been guilty of suspecting that he just wasn't listening?

For years I thought Grampa Dooly was stone deaf. He used to sit around in his sagging chair in his sagging work clothes and spit tobacco juice into a Prince Albert can. If he happened to have anything to say to you, he would yell loud enough to send the cat diving for cover under the sofa. I was disillusioned about Grampa one day when I heard my saintly (she really was) grandmother mutter, "He hears what he wants to hear." It was the only time I ever heard her mutter. I was impressed.

During the last forty years I've discovered that Grandma knew what she was talking about. Grampa wasn't the only male with this hearing problem. I've repeated myself so much that I've finally reached the point where I just automatically say everything twice. Otherwise, we have conversations like this:

"The potatoes will be ready in about twenty minutes," I say

to my husband, the outdoor chef. "Would you like to light the grill now?"

No response. Well, maybe he didn't hear. After all, he must be a full three feet away.

"Do you want to light the grill now, Dear?"

I look at him expectantly. Nothing.

Did you know that if you stare intently at someone, you'll get his attention? Sooner or later. Finally, he looks up. Uh-oh. Now he knows he's missed something.

"What's that?" he asks.

"You haven't heard a word I've said!"

"Oh, yes I did."

"What did I say?"

"I didn't catch it all. Something about a will. Did the lawyer call?"

"Not *will*, grill. GRILL! I thought you might want to light the grill now."

"Oh, is it time to light the grill? Why didn't you say so? All you had to do was ask."

I should be thankful. If he *had* caught the word "grill," he probably would have thought immediately of the car and assumed I'd had a close encounter of the metallic kind. Now *that* he would have heard.

Dinner is finally on the table and we're in mid-meal.

"Pass the salt, please," Greg asks.

The salt resides at Dad's right hand, where it remains untouched. Seconds tick away.

"Please pass the salt."

Still no reaction.

"Dad!"

Dad looks up, recognizes the glance between mother and son, and looks helplessly around for something to pass.

"Salt," I say.

Sorry, Miss Manners. We try, but sometimes it's easier just to reach. Or get up and walk around the table.

"I was not told." This icy and rather imperious response is evoked by the discovery of any flurry of activity or bit of news of which the man of the house slowly becomes aware—when he doesn't understand what's going on.

"But Dad, we talked about it for fifteen minutes. You were sitting *right there*."

"I was not told," he sniffs in an injured tone.

The town crier hired by the city of Pittsburgh during the newspaper strike is probably looking for work now. Maybe we should see if she's interested.

The first inkling I had of this Y-chromosome disability came when we brought our first baby, affectionately called The Howler, home from the hospital. This kid had a cry that would trigger the Richter Scale, and, at only five pounds, more endurance than an Olympic cross-country skier. For the first few weeks, the bassinet was in our bedroom, but you don't think old Rip V. Winkle had a clue that she never drew a quiet breath from midnight till daylight, do you?

That kind of sound repose may be "the sleep of the just," but it seems pretty unjust when you're jiggling a screaming infant and wearing a permanent path into a hardwood floor.

This male characteristic appears in childhood, but only in situations where someone is saying "take a bath" or "take out the garbage" or "go to bed." In adolescence, it becomes evident only when parents and teachers are speaking, although the necessity for playing music at astronomical decibel levels should give us a clue to the problem. Otherwise, it tends to increase sharply shortly after the wedding ceremony. What pre-marriage counselor ever thinks to tell the bride that "I do" is probably the last thing she says that her husband will hear?

Is the poor, hearing-impaired man not more to be pitied than censured? Does he not deserve our sympathy for having inherited, along with original sin, this unfortunate disability? Not when he can watch one baseball game and listen to two others at the same time. Not when he can simultaneously follow the intricacies of three bowl games on New Year's Day and not only know the scores, but he can also tell you the line of scrimmage, what down it is, and which commentator is speaking at any given moment.

Like most men, my husband can hear the tiniest ping in the engine of a car. He can hear the rustle of a box of chocolates being opened at a hundred yards. And I would swear that, long before the fragrance wafts through the house, he can hear a cake baking in the oven.

The other night the garage-door opener in his car was dead, and he had to trudge around the back of the house through a foot of snow to the kitchen door.

"I sat out there in the driveway and blew the horn for five minutes," he fumed.

"Sorry," I said. "I never heard a thing."

## nine

## Why Pray When You Can Worry?

Did you hear about the ninety-year-old woman who was rocking on the porch with her equally aged husband? She looked at him with a sigh of relief and said, "Well, honey, I guess we can stop worrying about the kids now. The last one just went on Social Security."

What is it with this fascination—almost an obsession—about having babies? Young girls want them, single men and women want them, childless couples want them, and for some totally inexplicable reason, some FIFTY-YEAR-OLD women want them. The problem with having babies is that once you have them, you *have* them. Twenty-four hours a day. Forever. So long as ye both shall live.

The minute the doctor says, "I have good news for you," (they always say that, no matter how welcome the news is at that particular moment) it starts. You have drawn your last peaceful breath.

If you are a parent, you will agree with me. If you're not, trust me. *You will never stop worrying about this child!* And unless some kind of perfect look-alike android from the Ideal Child Robotics Company is substituted for your offspring in the hospital nursery, this little bundle of joy will give you plenty to worry about. Throughout infancy, childhood, and adolescence. Long after he has come of age and become (it is to be hoped) gainfully employed. Whether he is halfway around the world or living next door. For the rest of his natural life. And yours.

You may have heard someone say, "I'll do my best until these kids are eighteen (or twenty-one, or out of school). After that, they're on their own." People who say such things probably have kids who are still in diapers. Wait until one of your own shows up on your doorstep with one of his/her own in diapers.

The Baby Boomer generation gets a lot of attention these days. What about the Baby *Boomeranger*—the ones who leave home at high speed and then turn around and head right back? These are the same kids who, at sixteen, daily announced to the world at large and to their parents in particular that "as soon as I'm eighteen I'm outta here!"

Over dessert in a restaurant the other night, a friend was talking about her twenty-five-year-old son's impending marriage. "Yes!" she exulted. "He's moving out!" So much for the Empty Nest Syndrome. Moving out is a whole lot easier the second time around. For everybody involved.

We talk tough, but the truth is that it really doesn't matter where the kids live. We still worry. When they are babies, we worry about everything. We worry if they cry, but we worry more if they don't cry. We tiptoe into the nursery in the middle of the night just to see if they are still breathing. But with infants, at least we don't wonder if they'll still be in the crib or playpen or wherever we left them. When the moment comes that we go back and discover Junior has hoisted himself out of the crib and made his escape, industrial-strength worrying kicks in.

When Junior becomes a toddler the main worry is (a) where he is and (b) what he is destroying at the moment. Constant vigilance is the price of survival for kids who will ingest any substance—animal, vegetable, or mineral. Why is it that the same little darlings who are discriminating enough to turn up their noses at strained beets and carrots do not hesitate to drink kerosene (my daughter) or bleach (my son). Thanks to early intervention and the unappetizing taste of these liquids, the quantities were small enough that the consequences were limited to a distinctive pungency during diaper-changing for a day or so.

When you have school-age children, you don't worry about whether an injury will occur. You're way beyond that by this time. It's just a question of which bone, muscle, or ligament is involved and whether stitches will be required. Forget about your standing appointment at the beauty shop. Make one at the emergency room of your local hospital. By the time the kid graduates from high school you will have accumulated enough crutches, slings, and Ace bandages to supply a M.A.S.H. unit.

Nothing, I repeat, NOTHING strikes fear into the heart of a parent like that last vestige of primitive Coming of Age rituals, the only one we have in modern American culture: Getting a Driver's License. Beyond the endless bickering over who drives whom, when, where, and in what, lie Technicolor, wide-screen visions of your vehicle smashed up on the interstate or lying mangled in a ditch somewhere along a lonely country road. Every ring of the telephone and every far-off whine of a siren triggers a panic attack. We're talking high-octane anxiety here. If anything can put tracks in a trackless carpet, it's waiting up to hear that car turn into the driveway an hour past curfew.

If you watch TV, listen to the radio, or read newspapers or magazines, you will quickly discover that you would really have to budget your time to find enough hours in the day to worry about all the stuff that could adversely affect your child's health, safety, and well-being. You need a schedule in order to fit in all the stuff you need to worry about: contaminants in food and water, AIDS, flammable clothing, second-hand smoke, asbestos and lead poisoning, teachers that favor boys over girls, drugs, making the football team/cheerleading squad, sexual harassment on the school bus (are wedgies and bra-snapping worthy of litigation?), SAT scores, acne and its effect on self-esteem, violence in the media, violent crime in McDonald's and the 7-Eleven and the post office, broken hearts, natural disasters, discrimination by everyone against everyone else, getting into the college of your choice, paying for the college (not necessarily of your choice) you can most nearly afford without declaring bankruptcy, dead batteries in the smoke alarm, the possibility of a disastrous marriage, the inexorable progress of the killer bees, and the likelihood that North Korea has nuclear capability. *To name a few.*

When my children were older and driving hundreds of miles

alone, back and forth from college, we did everything we could to insure a safe trip: car in good shape, AAA membership, daylight travel. Then I tried to stay so busy I didn't have time to think (too much) about it. Still, I hovered as close as possible to a telephone—just in case.

One cold Valentine's Day I grabbed the phone and answered it on the first ring. Christi was driving home to Pennsylvania from Nashville.

"Mom?"

"What's wrong?" (typical mother's response).

"Nothing now." She knew enough to calm me down and assure me that everything was cool before attempting to explain about the flat tire that had stranded her on the side of I-65 in Kentucky. It was pouring rain and she was so sore she could hardly walk, the result of sitting on the front row at a basketball game and getting bowled over and knocked out cold by a 6'6" forward a couple of days earlier. But no police cars appeared and no one seemed inclined to stop, so she decided she would have to start walking.

Just as she got out of the car, a big sedan pulled up. The driver was a middle-aged woman.

I interrupted the narrative. Any mother would have to. "You didn't get in the car with a stranger!"

"It's OK, Mom," Christi assured me.

And it was OK. Her rescuer was not only a Christian lady, but a member of our own denomination (which isn't a large one), and even knew some of Christi's college classmates.

A fortunate coincidence? I don't think so.

Velma, our Good Samaritan, drove this road five days a week and knew exactly how long it took to get to work. On this day, *for some reason,* she started out fifteen minutes early. She had no idea why. But I do. And she was right on time.

Incidentally, I tried to locate our rescuer by making phone calls to church leaders and enlisting the help of a friend in the area who was sure she could find anyone who fit the description. No luck. Hmmm. Could that Good Samaritan have been a guardian angel...?

"Well, Mom," Christi said, once she was safely home. "It's nice to know this prayer stuff really works." What she *didn't* say was, "Your worrying really paid off." She knew me well enough to know I had been doing more than worrying, and we both knew which endeavor had proved more effective.

"Fret not," David said in Psalm 37. Goodness knows, he had plenty to fret about and had in fact done his share. But he also knew how futile, pointless, non-productive, and totally exhausting it is. The things you worry about never seem to happen, and when trouble does come, it usually arrives in a form that takes us by surprise.

From the recesses of my childhood memory (which is better than my middle-aged memory), I recall a sprightly little chorus all about cheering up and having faith because there is nothing to worry or be fearful about, and warning that we'll be sorry tomorrow that we worried today. Ideally and ultimately, of course, that is true. But humanly and realistically, everybody—especially parents—knows there are plenty of things that can make us fretful, fearful, and doubtful. David ended Psalm 37 by saying, "The Lord will help them... because they trust in him." I guess he ought to know!

A pastor once concluded a sermon on faith with this fervent but accidental admonition to the congregation: "Remember, why pray when you can worry?"

And too many of God's people said, "Amen."

# ten

## Coping with Mr. Clean

In our best moments of clear-eyed honesty, we have to admit that we let ourselves in for a lot of frustration through our efforts to do and to be, to please and achieve. Even when it's not our fault that things go wrong and stuff breaks down, we tend to blame ourselves. Result? Stress. But that's not the whole story. A lot of it is brought about by that large segment of society known as Other People.

Other People come in all shapes, colors, sizes, and denominations. They don't think like we do. Other People act weird, get in our way, take up our time, and make demands on our resources. Other People can be surly waiters, indifferent doctors, rude salesclerks, or impatient customers. At home, Other People may look perfectly normal or perhaps take the form of a shaved-head, nose-pierced son, a daughter who is into tattoos, or simply the classic clothes-on-the-floor, toothpaste-squeezed-in-the-middle, leave-the-toilet-seat-up spouse.

What can you do about the eccentricities, idiosyncracies, irritating behavior, and annoying habits of Other People? Not a lot. Wait for them to grow up or mellow out. Marshal all your defense mechanisms and learn to cope. And you can always complain.

As a long-suffering member of a silent minority, I have finally decided to speak up—to come out of the broom closet—and respond to all those women who bellyache about messy husbands. You think you've got problems? OK, maybe you do. But believe me, it's no picnic being married to "Mr. Clean."

When I was growing up, I never doubted for a minute that some day my knight in shining armor would come riding into my life. I never dreamed that when he finally arrived, he would turn out to be a combination of the White Knight and the Tidy Bowl Man.

Looking back on our courtship, remembering those spit-shined penny loafers, chinos with finely-honed creases, and the mirror-like finish of that '58 green-and-white Chevy Impala, I realize I should have been prepared. Nevertheless, I was somewhat taken aback, a few months into marriage, by a comment about the unsightly state of the top of our refrigerator. Really. Who can even *see* the top of the refrigerator?

Here's a recent episode of "Lifestyles of the Clean and Spotless" that shows how much I've learned since those early days:

I had been speaking at an all-day workshop, and "Mr. C" and some friends met me in Pittsburgh at a nice restaurant for dinner that evening.

"Guess what I did today!" he exclaimed as soon as we were seated.

"You did a bleach job on the kitchen counter," I replied, never glancing up from my menu.

"Yep," he answered gleefully. "You should have seen all those black marks under the Cuisinart!"

Our friends weren't even pretending to read their menus, but were watching and listening in amusement—or was it amazement? How could I possibly have guessed a thing like that?

It wasn't a guess. I knew. If the man wasn't sloshing Clorox all over, he would spend an hour ruthlessly forcing tiny curls of gunk at knifepoint from around the edge of the sink.

As a means of survival in the early years of marriage, I quickly learned to adapt. If I had chosen to spend the day sewing or shopping or loafing at the pool, all I had to do was put the vacuum cleaner in the middle of the floor, hide the dirty dishes in the oven, and spray a little Lemon Pledge in the air. When Mr. Clean arrived, I was sure to win the Good Housekeeping in Progress Seal of Approval!

The children also had to do their share of coping. Consider this typical scenario:

It's a warm, sunny day. The kids have just finished washing my car. Dad pulls into the driveway.

"How's it look, Dad?"

"Great! Nice job!" His lips are smiling, but his eyes are riveted on a streak on the windshield while one sleeve surreptitiously rubs a tiny smudge on the fender.

Fortunately, the children understand. They assume it's genetic, having observed since early childhood their aunts' and grandmother's uncompromising observance of the annual Rites of Spring Cleaning. During these pre-Lenten rituals, Grandma's house was entirely denuded, and every single item washed, dirty or not. No vase, doily, picture, windowpane, or wall escaped—no matter that you couldn't tell where you had stopped or started and the water in your pail didn't even change color. If I go to the effort of scrubbing something, I like to see where I've been and where I'm going! Otherwise, forget it.

This genetic theory is supported by the cleaning habits of an octogenarian aunt who, without the slightest qualm, walked a plank placed across two stepladders while she Spic-and-Spanned all the ceilings in the house. Her basement floor was cleaner than—well, cleaner than some folks' refrigerator tops!

Mr. C's relentless enthusiasm turns garage-cleaning, cellar-cleaning, and barn-cleaning into much-dreaded ordeals for those members of the family who happened to miss out on that tidiness trait in the gene pool. At these marathon sessions, Mr. Clean wages all-out battle. He sees dirt as the Enemy and himself as the Enforcer. In his hands, a broom becomes a lethal weapon. He really ought to have a license to operate the thing.

Being married to Mr. Clean also involves traveling with Mr. Clean. This presents its own set of challenges. Motels and restaurants are carefully scrutinized. First impressions are crucial.

We were taking a leisurely trip to New England to relax and

enjoy the fall foliage—or so I thought—and it was time to stop for the night.

"But the travel book gave it three stars!" I wailed as he peered at the front of the motel then sped off into the darkness. It was late and I was tired.

"I don't care. I'd drive all night before I'd stay there."

We almost did.

If the *Guiness Book of World Records* had a category called "Brief Motel Stays," I'm sure we would top the list. One time we hauled all our luggage into a room of a national chain, then he pulled down the bedspread, looked at the pillows, and announced, "We're checking out."

And we did.

In restaurants, cleanliness takes precedence over cuisine. Silverware is carefully scrutinized, salt and pepper shakers checked for grease and fingerprints. By the way, would you be interested in helping to drum up support for a Constitutional Amendment requiring all cooks and waitresses (and some waiters) to wear hair nets? Mr. Clean would be grateful—and so would I.

The irresistible urge to run a finger across any horizontal surface extends to the office, where the real bottom line is the amount of dust on the philodendron.

To be perfectly fair, I must acknowledge that there are occasional benefits. We were having a late snack one evening, and Mr. C. was getting ice cubes from the freezer. "Check the top of the refrigerator," I said.

As he ran his hand over its smooth, polished surface, his pleasure was evident and my efforts well rewarded. Move over, Total Woman. I've got a few tricks of my own. Who needs the fragrance of Obsession when you've got Murphy's Oil Soap?

I have no doubt that this passion for the pristine will also prove to be eternal. If cleanliness is indeed next to godliness, I'm sure Mr. Clean will be rewarded with a sizeable establishment in heaven. There's an old gospel song that says, "Angels,

Get My Mansion Ready." I just hope those housekeeping angels do a thorough job. The occupant will no doubt arrive wearing white gloves, checking for any specks of gold dust that may have drifted in from the streets and settled on the harp strings.

In heaven, of course, we will no longer ponder the paradoxes of human nature. But until that time, I can't help wondering how a person who scrubs his golf clubs with a toothbrush after every single use can leave wrenches and screwdrivers lying wherever they were last used. How can someone who delights in spotless, shining table tops and counters feel no compunction about strewing those surfaces with letters, papers, and pocket accumulata? And the real puzzler: How can a man who showers twice a day insist on going outdoors in an ancient, grease-strained, grime-encrusted jacket that hangs—quite literally—in shreds and is fit only for the incinerator? Go figure.

Could it be that the King James Version has St. Peter translated with perfect accuracy and that we are, indeed, a *peculiar* people? And that these very characteristics—our human faults and foibles and inconsistencies—become, through the years, our most endearing and memorable qualities?

People who live together, it is said, tend to become more and more alike over the years. Some observers have even suggested that husbands and wives start to look alike. Others simply say that alterations occur in ideas, attitudes, and habits. When a lark marries an owl, for example, they tend to compromise on times for rising and retiring.

I don't know where this theory came from, but I think it's absurd. How could anyone possibly absorb any characteristics of a neatnik just by living with him for a long time? I find it highly unlikely.

And now, if you will excuse me, I'm feeling a strange urge to go and wax the garage floor. I'd better lie down until it goes away.

## eleven

## The Great Christmas Flush-out and Other Holiday Memories

"...Be of good cheer, for Christmas comes but once a year." And a good thing it is, too. Most of us get about all the good cheer we can handle during that ill-defined and constantly expanding period known as the "holiday season." Five months of unrelenting jollity gets pretty wearing. The only people I can think of who wish Christmas came around more often are retailers and psychiatrists—and, naturally, kids.

'Tis the season for festive family dinners and parties that absolutely ooze with togetherness. 'Tis the season for Kodak Moments. 'Tis the season when credit cards go into massive overload. 'Tis the season for making enough memories and observing enough traditions for Shirley Dobson and Gloria Gaither to write another book about.

'Tis also the season for waxing nostalgic over things that never happened. Have you ever dashed through the snow in a one-horse open sleigh? How many people do you know who have ever tasted a chestnut, let alone roasted one on an open fire? Just try decking the halls with holly—the real stuff, I mean. It's vicious. Your hands will feel like they were attacked by a demented acupuncturist. And if you've never hung real mistletoe, don't bother. The plastic stuff produces the same results, and it's not poisonous.

I'll tell you what 'tis the season for, and you won't find it in any Christmas songs, old or new. 'Tis the season for stress.

Stress, the experts tell us, is caused by change. It is most often triggered by disruptions in one's lifestyle: a change in marital status, additions and losses within the family, alteration in living arrangements. Job changes, whether you got fired or promoted. Up or down, it's still stressful.

How do I know all this? Research. Scientific studies. And where are these reports to be found? Women's magazines. They overflow with advice on how to cope. But what these ubiquitous periodicals unfailingly fail to mention is that *it's all their fault.*

No sooner are the watermelons off these magazine covers than the seductive holiday issues appear at the supermarket checkout. You've seen them—the ones featuring a gigantic roasted turkey, stuffed with cornbread and walnuts, slathered with butter, and sporting a tan that would be the envy of the cover girl on the *Sports Illustrated* swimsuit issue. Glorious vegetable dishes, enticing enough to get George Bush to eat broccoli, are nestled up against death-defying desserts. Just looking at these concoctions makes your fat cells quiver in anticipation and your cholesterol shoot up forty points. Inside these magazines, of course, are nutritionally correct recipes for tofu-and-crushed-Melba-toast stuffing and ricecake-yogurt pudding. Try serving that to your family and see what happens to peace and goodwill.

So what does all this have to do with stress? I told you. It creates it! You see all that gorgeous food with its elegant "presentation" and you think, "I can do that." It starts as a nice idea which soon turns into an obligation and ends up a mild obsession. So there you are at three o'clock Christmas morning, strung out and bleary-eyed, cutting out little frilled paper booties for the turkey to wear to the dinner table.

Still, it's not the recipes that put me over the edge. It's all those articles with titles like "How to Have an Excruciatingly Perfect Christmas with Absolutely No Effort on Your Part." I have garnered a number of incredibly helpful suggestions designed to de-stress the holiday, which I am happy to share in case you missed them.

1. *Set the table several days ahead of time.* Great idea. You can eat out for a week.
2. *Clean in advance.* This plan is most effective when kids are locked outside until bedtime. The neighbors have bathrooms. (We once lived across the street from a woman who actually did that.)
3. *Bake ahead.* Now this sounds like a really good idea until you realize it involves going through your recipe file (read "shoebox") and discovering that all your family favorites have been hijacked by Tinker Bell to Never-Never Land. (These very recipes will miraculously reappear on January 3.) It means making lists of ingredients and then somehow managing to get those lists into the grocery store and actually locating the items on the shelves. If your supermarket is like mine, they wait until you finally figure out where those fancy little toothpicks are before calling in all the part-time help to rearrange every item in the store. By the time you get home, you're exhausted and you haven't even started looking for the rolling pin. But make sure you find it—it could come in handy later on!
4. *Freeze everything.* Listen, once something is shrouded in white and stashed away in my freezer, it's headed for mummification. If it ever does see the light of day, it tastes about as fresh as that food they found in King Tut's tomb. And don't think you can pass off snowman cookies as next fall's pumpkins. It won't work. Trust me.
5. *Delegate responsibility.* The first suggestion is usually to make a chore chart. Now that's a major chore in itself, and you know who gets to do it. (Don't forget to give someone the job of dusting all that china that's been sitting out for a week.) Leave cleaning supplies and sponges by the sink for guests to clean up after themselves. Now, that would spruce up your holiday decor. Maybe you could make little holly-sprigged hats for the Lysol and Sani-Flush.

There's more, but you get the idea: given enough time, endless preparation, innumerable lists, and unlimited cooperation from family, you could plan your way to a perfect, stress-free yuletide holiday. Sure. And Elvis will show up and sing "Blue Christmas."

"The best-laid plans of mice and men," said Scottish poet Robert Burns more than two hundred years ago, "go oft awry." (Actually he said "gang aft a-gley," but those words aren't in my computer's spell-check so I changed them.)

Old Bobbie Burns was right on. You can take every bit of advice in every magazine on the market—everything your mother taught you, the complete text of *Hints from Heloise*, and get a blood transfusion from Martha Stewart—and still not be prepared for the things that *really* happen when families get together to celebrate the holidays. Take, for instance, what has come to be known in our family as The Great Christmas Flush-Out. (Not to be confused with The Great Christmas Flood. More about that later.)

This particular Christmas, for once, I felt truly prepared. Well, almost prepared. The house was clean, the gifts wrapped, baking completed, ham browning nicely in the oven. The kids sat cozily in front of the crackling fireplace, playing Aggravation—which I should have interpreted as foreshadowing. It was a scene to make Norman Rockwell reach for his brush and palette.

A car turned into the driveway and we ran to the door. "Merry Christmas! Come in," I greeted our guests. "I hope you don't plan to take a shower or use the bathroom for the next few days."

My brother and his family, like the Magi, had traveled from afar bearing gifts. They had two choices: come in or turn around and drive eight hundred miles back home on Christmas Eve. They came in.

Sorry, folks, but this house *is* a hundred years old. You expect country charm *and* functional plumbing?

Why not call a plumber? Get real. On holidays plumbers are scarcer than archbishops at a Kentucky camp meeting.

None of those oh-so-helpful magazine articles had even hinted at anything like this. Actually, I had ever-so-slightly exaggerated our situation. Through the combined efforts of father and son and our good neighbor Jack, along with an unattractive but amazingly useful implement known affectionately as a "snake," the downstairs bathroom was marginally and temporarily functional.

It was not a situation to foster good cheer, however. Our objective was clear; it was time to gather the troops and lay out a strategic plan. That accomplished, we scattered throughout the house to see that sinks and bathtubs were filled to the brim. Then men went outside and headed "down over the hill" (our euphemism for the place where Erma Bombeck says the grass is always greener), while the women and children assumed battle stations throughout the house. From my post at an upstairs window, my task was to watch and listen, Paul-Revere-like, until I picked up the prearranged signal. "Go!" I echoed the cry, which we passed along from room to room like an Olympic torch. Simultaneously, plug-pullers pulled and flushers flushed. The house took one huge, gurgling gulp.

Back at the window, I anxiously awaited a sign from the front lines. The fellows climbed over the fence and high-fived each other. Success! We had routed the plumbing grinch who had threatened to steal our Christmas. Good will (and profound relief) flowed as freely as the drains.

So much for the Flush. A few years later came the Flood. I knew things were "ganging agley" bigtime that cold Christmas Eve when I ran down to the kitchen to start breakfast. Squish, squish. Icy water engulfed my bare feet. My holiday plans had definitely not included a broken water pipe in—where else?—the most inaccessible place in the kitchen. Neither had I planned to spend the entire day walking around displaced cabinets and appliances, not to mention two pairs of legs protruding from the inner recesses of the cupboards. I didn't hear any ho-ho-ho's from the owners of the legs, either. Although I got quite a few laughs later, from the pictures I took!

The Flush. The Flood. And then the Fire. It's starting to sound downright biblical!

Anyway, one Christmas Eve the dishwasher caught fire. Now tell me how you plan for a thing like that. You've got fourteen people in the house for a week—*that's* what you've been planning for, not a cloud of smoke that bursts into flame when you open the dishwasher door. How could you know that a toddler with a passion for ping-pong balls would choose to deposit one in the dishwasher right before the door was closed? A ping-pong ball is no problem during the wash cycle, but when that little yellow ball comes to rest on the heating element... you wouldn't believe the smoke. Then, when the door is opened and flames erupt... panic. Fortunately, the fire burned itself out, but by that time, so had my nerves!

I'm probably the only person in the Christian community who thinks of the hymn that says, "some through the water, some through the flood, some through the fire..." as a Christmas carol.

My son Greg and I were working upstairs the other day, taking up some old carpet. He was prying up the nailstudded strips of wood from around the baseboard, and one section was splintering badly.

"Oops," he said, as a few fragments tumbled down the open furnace duct. "That won't cause any trouble, will it?"

"I don't think so," I said. "I doubt if it will catch on fire."

"Well, if it does," my experienced son replied, "you know when it will happen. Christmas."

So young and so cynical. I have found it reassuring, however, to discover that I'm *not* the only one who has had to deal with some truly unexpected Christmas surprises. If you're interested....

Ask some people I know, who went off to Christmas Eve

services and came back to find all their carefully wrapped presents totally trashed by a malcontented family dog.

Ask my brother and sister-in-law, who found that their tall fir tree mysteriously grew three feet on the trip home. The evergreen monster was so tall and so heavy they couldn't even get the thing to stand up, let alone into a tree stand and inside the house. (It looked so much smaller out in the countryside with all the other trees!) The Hanging of the Greens takes on a new perspective when it requires the use of a ingeniously improvised rope-and-pulley contraption. In case you ever need to hoist an oversized tree to an upright position, I'm sure they could give you detailed instructions.

Ask a couple who always wait to put up the tree until Christmas Eve after the kids are in bed. They will gladly tell you about the year they decided that a *revolving* tree would be a nice surprise. Was it ever. As it turned out, the motor had just a tad too much torque. If you want the whole story, ask their kids about having to dodge ornaments flying in all directions like misguided missiles, sending them scurrying for safety behind the furniture. If the cat could talk, it might tell you why it stays clear of any room with a tree in it.

Can you ever really "get ready" for Christmas? I doubt it. No matter how much planning and preparing, there is always something that just didn't get done. How important can it be? None of this really has anything to do with the arrival of Christmas. When Christmas comes, it just comes. Silently, often when we least expect it, the beauty and wonder and joy of the season slip quietly into our souls, and we know it's Christmas.

One Christmas not long ago, for a number of reasons, the spirit of the season had eluded me. The celebrations seemed superficial, the lights gaudy, the music tinny, the shopping tiresome. But then one cold evening as I stood in an overheated, over-decorated store, gazing rather helplessly around the men's department, a phrase from a Muzak carol somehow managed to penetrate my gloom: "and man shall live forevermore because of Christmas Day."

I knew that. And that was all that really mattered. Suddenly, without any effort on my part, right there between the light-up reindeer boxer shorts and the "Bah, Humbug" sweatshirts, Christmas came to my heart.

# twelve

## Y'all Come See Us

"Y'all come!" was the motto of my childhood. In the South, "having comp'ny" was a frequent and usually welcome break in the family routine. For us kids, it sometimes meant getting out of regular chores. But even if there were more dishes to wash, there would be somebody to pitch in and help you get them done. You handed your guests a dish towel just as matter-of-factly as you gave them the best piece of chicken. The table was crowded but nobody cared, unless there were so many that the youngest got relegated to the kitchen. I'd rather be squeezed on the piano bench with two other kids and elbows in my ribs than miss those privileged glimpses into the grown-up world that dinner-table talk provided. It was fascinating.

Making places for everybody at the table was easy compared to finding sleeping accommodations. It usually meant putting the younger children on pallets made of quilts on the floor. I can't recall anyone complaining—not that it would have done any good. Personally, I loved it. If you played possum, you could listen to the adults talking late into the night—another peek into the mysterious realm of adulthood. In those pre-TV days, children were children. We were seldom privy to adult discussions, blissfully ignorant of adult problems and passions. It made for a secure, if rather dull, childhood. A little eavesdropping now and then was a heady experience.

The importance of "company" was evident in our vocabulary: everybody had company dishes (the ones without the chips), company dinner menus (dessert a certainty), and company linens (starched pillowcases with crocheted trim). We didn't have anything worthy of the name "parlor," but "front rooms" were reserved for entertaining company. We kids even had company manners, which basically involved behaving—an undefined yet clearly understood set of expectations.

Usually our "comp'ny" was relatives—an interesting lot, especially the ones who drove up in big Buicks or Packards, with their cigarette cases and gold lighters and vocabularies that we were definitely not accustomed to hearing. I was partial to the traveling evangelists, who were as good at getting us to laugh at their stories as they were at getting people to come to the altar. Their hilarious tales, some of them no doubt embellished in the telling, about the people in the churches and homes they had visited in their travels would have provided many of them a second career in stand-up comedy. At the time it didn't occur to me that they might go off and tell other people how ridiculous we were.

My very favorite visitors were college students. They came from church colleges in quartets or trios, singing and doing PR during the summer. I admired them enormously and wanted to be just like them. They were friendly and funny, joking about their travels and telling embarrassing stories about their professors, including the one with whom they were traveling. The guys liked to say that they had trouble getting laundry done, so they wore their socks until they stuck when thrown at the wall. I found that highly amusing. But not nearly as amusing as I suspect they found us, especially when they went back to tell about the comfort facilities in our rural parsonage. There were none. We had five rooms and a path.

Outhouses were still common in some remote areas in the fifties, but our outhouse was an uncommon one. It had no door. Before too many mental images emerge, let me explain. It was located behind the barn, so close that there was just room to slip inside. No one could see inside, so who needed a door? In fact, there wasn't even room for a door. The only real problem was that there was no way to see if the facility was occupied. (It was just a one-holer. Did you know that Abraham Lincoln's home in Springfield is a two-holer; but Wheatfield, the home of President Buchanan, had *five?* In a row. In graduated sizes, like pearls on a string. But I digress.) In our little doorless necessary house, the best the occupant could do was listen for footsteps, then have a fit of coughing or find it advisable to clear the throat loudly enough to issue a warning.

The outhouse was quite a distance from the house, which presented the potential user the added disadvantage of not being able to look out and see if the nonexistent door was open. To avoid the inconvenience of fruitless trips, Daddy came up with an ingenious idea. He nailed a piece of red cloth to a short length of wood, and then nailed the resulting flag to the corner of the barn. When you rounded the corner on your way in, you simply put the flag up. Anyone could see from the house whether it was worth a trip. But woe be upon anyone who went about his business (if you'll pardon the expression) and forgot to put the flag down. Every time company came, we had the privilege of explaining the system to them. Everybody thought it was a real hoot. I've always wondered how much mileage those college kids got out of telling that story. A lot, I would imagine.

No one is sorry that we have moved beyond all those primitive arrangements. We coddle our houseguests with hideabeds, guest rooms, and indoor plumbing all over the house. Even air conditioning. But things have changed. Something has happened to the easygoing hospitality of an earlier generation. Saying "Y'all come," today, in my experience, is a one-way ticket to stress, exhaustion, and quite possibly household disaster.

I really must check with Miss Manners to discover the correct course of action to take when friends are visiting and everyone has retired and a resounding crash from the guest room announces that the bed has fallen in. Do you pretend you didn't hear? Do you rush to see if anyone is injured? Dial 911? Wait until somebody yells "help"? Offer to repair the damage immediately or just let them sleep on the floor? It's happened to us more than once. I've never gotten around to looking under "bed-busting" in an etiquette book, but even if there did happen to be a proper way to handle it, it would still be monumentally embarrassing!

Years ago, nothing ever seemed to go wrong when guests were in the house. But in my household, if any appliance is going to break down, that's when it will happen. My sister was here one summer with her five kids. Nine of us for a week. Guess when the water line had to be repaired. I'm talking ditches in the yards and all new pipes. Another time it was the dishwasher. Then the dryer. Can the furnace be far behind?

Earlier this week, the day before overnight guests were expected, I opened the door under the sink and discovered a coat of chewed-up vegetable matter plastering the cupboard like damp stucco. The garbage disposal had somehow disengaged itself from the drainpipe, disgorged its contents, and breathed its last. Not again!

By now I'm a seasoned veteran of appliance emergencies, and I know what to do. *Leave it alone.* Don't touch it. Mankind flourished disposal-less for centuries. We can manage for a few days. So when my husband announced that the electrician would be coming at nine o'clock the next morning, I went ballistic. Ed was calm and reassuring. Not to worry. He was just going to check the switch. If that wasn't the problem, nothing would be done. OK. This was the guy who always came when we needed him and had just the week before restored our electricity after a severe storm knocked out several circuits. (Last year we were hit by lightning which took out our central air conditioning, VCR, answering machine, and two TVs, but that's another story.) Anyway, I trusted him.

Mr. Repairman arrived on schedule and found nothing wrong with the switch.

"We'll just let it go for now," I said.

"Well, I don't understand why that reset button won't pop out. I'll just take this bottom plate off. I hate to leave a job without accomplishing anything." He started in with the screwdriver.

A few minutes later, I walked back into the kitchen. The disposal was out on the floor, drains unconnected.

"I can't get it back in there," our helper announced. "I don't know anything about these things," he confided. "Never worked on them before."

I had trouble listening to the diagnosis while trying to remember what is it you're supposed to do when you start to hyperventilate. It appeared that the motor was shot. So why put it back in? A few quick calls located a new disposal. Good news: it would be delivered to our door in fifteen minutes.

Bad news: our electrical friend had to leave—just for a little while, he said. The new disposal arrived, but no one was there to install it. The sink was useless. I couldn't run water. I couldn't cook. I couldn't clean up the mess. Guests' e.t.a. is 1:00 P.M. It is now past noon.

Like the cavalry riding over the hill in an old western movie, help arrived—with reinforcements—just in the nick of time. Pipes were reattached. Everything worked. I could begin to prepare lunch, except for one minor difficulty. In all the confusion of the morning, no one had time to go to the grocery. Oh well, it was getting pretty late. By that time they would have eaten.

Wrong! They were hungry. I should have known. The typical male "drive to arrive" had precluded any possibility of stopping for a sandwich. I had not one slice of bread in the house. But I had baked the day before, so—voila!—I borrowed Marie Antoinette's solution for the starving people of Paris: Let them eat cake! Best cake they ever ate, it turned out to be. Must have the recipe. Shoot, it wasn't that great. They were just that hungry.

We're supposed to extend hospitality not only to our friends, the Bible says, but also to strangers, who just might be angels passing through the neighborhood. All I can say is that "angelic" doesn't exactly describe some of the strangers whom we have entertained from time to time. One case in point is a young woman, the friend of a relative, who spent some holiday time with us. It was the first time I ever saw anyone over the age of two snatch food right out of someone else's hand and eat it herself. At breakfast, everyone watched in astonishment while she kept stacking pancakes on her plate, oblivious to the fact that half the family had not been served. I had to run out to the kitchen and make more before the platter (which had been piled high) got all the way around the table. She picked quarrels, never lifted a finger to help, and then declared—in a decidedly uncomplimentary way—that she had never met people like us in her whole life!

I was frying bacon one morning, preparing breakfast for a guest speaker at our church the night before. Suddenly, the grease began to splatter. I looked up. Water was dripping from the ceiling into the skillet. That was clearly no angel in the upstairs bathroom. Now what should I do? Being well-bred, I was taught, requires one to ignore the gaffes of guests. I was on the verge of doing something really tacky—like banging on the door and yelling at the idiot to put the shower curtain inside the tub before he drowned his own breakfast and destroyed my ceiling tile—when the flood abated. The bacon was saved, and so was my dignity. And his.

The tradition of Southern hospitality in which I was raised does not always permit revealing the raw and unvarnished truth. One must never give the slightest hint that entertaining on any scale creates the slightest inconvenience. "It was no trouble at all," is the only proper attitude to take.

One of these days I'm going to be old enough to wear purple and eccentric enough to speak the truth. Perhaps, with practice, I can be as frank as one dignified Southern lady was when a friend of mine, leaving a formal reception, expressed appreciation for the invitation: "Well," her hostess replied with a sigh, "it was a lot of trouble, but I wanted to do it.

"Y'all come back now, y'hear?"

# part three

## The Patience Principle

Is it not enough to try the patience of men? **Isaiah 7:13**

PATIENCE IN CRITICAL CONDITION! Have you ever wished you could call your friendly family doctor and say, "Write me a prescription for patience—and please do it *right now*!" If only we could pop a patience pill, we could spare ourselves an awful lot of Maalox moments. Such, alas, is not the case. Everyday annoyances pester us like flies at a watermelon cutting. People, machines, animals, the forces of nature, the powers that be, and the U.S. Postal Service all unite to try to turn us into hair-tearing, nail-biting, floor-pacing, vein-throbbing basket cases. But remember, just because they are all out to get you is no reason to be paranoid. If aggravation seems to be your lot in life, cheer up. You are not alone.

# thirteen

## On the Road Again

We had really lucked out this time—four tickets to the Baseball All-Star Game in Pittsburgh. Along with our sports-loving friends Dick and Ellen, we were buzzing along I-79 on a sunny July afternoon. Dick had volunteered to drive his van, which Ellen had loaded with snacks and soft drinks. Suddenly, the hum of the pavement turned into a strange whine, and then we heard the unmistakable thlop-thlop of a flat tire.

Oh, well. Not to worry. We had plenty of room to pull off the road and plenty of time before the game. And nestled between the front seats was that sweet little miracle of modern technology—a cellular phone.

All in all, I declared, highly satisfactory circumstances in which to experience car trouble. So what if it took AAA almost an hour to arrive? So what if we had to limp along on a "doughnut" spare tire? This little roadside adventure barely deserved the name.

*Real* car trouble is having a flat tire on a horse trailer in rush-hour traffic in a strange town with no one who carries the tire-changing gene in sight. Real car trouble is a blowout on the interstate in holiday-weekend traffic that must be dodged in order to retrieve the hubcap that went flying like a crazed Frisbee and lodged against the guardrail. Even a late afternoon flat—two women alone—turns into real car trouble when the patrolman who drove by and actually stopped can't "give you a hand"—because he has a *broken* hand! You start to get the picture.

Our first experience of being truly and traumatically stranded was not out in the middle of nowhere, but just outside

Atlanta in six lanes of Friday night traffic. Ironically, we had just stopped to call my brother Raymond and say, "We're almost there." A houseful of friends and relatives were waiting to greet us. Minutes later, the car quit. Dead. In the hour that we waited while Ed went for help, not one car stopped—or even slowed down—and not one police car was in evidence. We might as well have been in the middle of the Arizona desert. Finally, a tow truck appeared and dragged us away to a service station that had no mechanic and couldn't do a thing to help us. By the time Raymond came to get us, another hour had passed, and by the time we arrived—the bedraggled guests of honor—the party was pretty much over! To make our long-awaited vacation complete, we had to pay yet another tow bill, do without a car for a week, and spring for a new engine. "Happy motoring!"

When you drive a big old International Travelall, known around town affectionately (or not) as the "Yellow Bomb," I guess you ought not to be too surprised when it gives you trouble. I had just pulled into a showground after a seven-hour trip with kids, tack, suitcases, and a two-horse trailer when it suddenly choked, gasped, and collapsed into an automotive coma. Everybody pitched in, unloaded, and went about their business, leaving me to cope—alone—with the Bomb. A big red truck arrived and a semi-helpful driver towed me away to parts unknown. Naturally, there was no mechanic at the station where I was taken. There never is. I was helpless in the hands of semi-interested attendants who assured me that someone with some idea of what might possibly be done would be back sometime that afternoon. Eventually, after much head-shaking and tsk-tsking, the diagnosis was that we (the Yellow Bomb and I) must be hauled off to yet another garage several miles out in the open country where there was a mechanic who would perhaps condescend to open the hood and take a peek inside. Of course, he wasn't there but was expected back—sometime.

I waited, wishing I had been as sensible as Hansel and Gretel and dropped some crumbs or pebbles along the way to guide me on my return journey. It was getting late, and I was getting worried when Mr. Mechanic finally appeared. I don't know what he did, but he opened the hood, jiggled things around, and in a few minutes had the old Bomb purring. I produced some plastic money and ventured out into the darkness. I wasn't sure where I was, where I had been, or how to find my way back. And it didn't help my mental or emotional state to know that the rest of our group was probably scarfing down steaks or soaking in the motel hot tub by that time.

Another episode in the continuing saga of "Adventures in Driving" occurred in heavy Pittsburgh traffic one day when my faithful and utterly dependable Chevy went into a Chinese dragon act and starting breathing white clouds of smoke. I glanced down and saw that the red temperature light was on, the needle all the way over on HOT. Holding my breath, I eased into the mall parking lot and coasted to a stop just as the engine expired. Relax, I told myself. *No need to panic. It's early in the day. You've got AAA. Keep your appointment. After all, it's not often you get a facial/manicure as a gift. Just enjoy it and worry about the car later.*

Sure. It's hard to relax and get your frown lines rubbed away when you're thinking about that hour's drive between you and home and just how serious your car's ailment might be. Finally, the facial was over and I could call for help. It would be an hour, everybody assured me, before help arrived. Go ahead with the manicure. I tried. It was too nerve-wracking. You can't chew your nails while somebody is clipping your cuticles.

I gave up and excused myself without benefit of polish and hurried back to the car. Look. See the wrecker. See the wrecker pulling away. See me run. Run, run, run. Scream. Scream loudly. Attract the attention of everyone in the parking lot... except the driver of the wrecker, of course.

I finally managed to catch him, but he might as well have

gone on his merry way. He couldn't do anything but tow me away. Why not just go to the auto service center across the mall parking lot? The car started, and the driver assured me I could travel a few hundred feet without going up in flames. I made him follow me anyway.

Three hours later, the car was still sitting right where I left it. We'll get to it, the manager assured me. Another hour. Closing time. Are you sure you're going to get to this tonight? No problem, I was told.

I peeked at the work order. Thermostat. That won't take long. Finally someone in work clothes with his name embroidered on the pocket stuck his head under the hood. I was encouraged. A few minutes later I was presented a bill for seventy-nine cents and told that a clamp was all that was needed. It was after 10:00 P.M.

Gratefully, I climbed in the car and headed for home. Five minutes later, the temperature was climbing. Another mile, and the car was steaming again. So was I. I pulled into a restaurant parking lot and called home for rescue. I ordered tea and waited. Another hour.

Ed decided to follow me as far as we could get. We limped along and finally abandoned the car at a market about halfway, and we got home well after midnight. The next day, after the car was repaired, I got the diagnosis. It needed a thermostat.

All these adventures, however, pale in comparison with our memorable Lexington Trip. The Yellow Bomb was overloaded this time, and pulling the trailer. Thankfully, I was not driving. In the Bomb, with all the luggage and tack, were three teenage girls: our daughter Christi, her cousin Jill, and her friend Vivian. We were looking forward to the Kentucky Horse Park and the show. The weather was fine. It would be a great weekend.

About half an hour from home, the rear end went out on the Yellow Bomb. It was its death knell. There we were, stranded with all our gear. And two horses.

A couple of hours later, we were re-loaded and on the road again—this time in my car, which fortunately was equipped with a trailer hitch. Not ten minutes down the road, smoke began to roll out from under the hood. An exit was coming up, and for once there was no debate about whether to take it. We made a rather hasty stop at a service station.

"Get away from the gas pumps," an attendant yelled while another called the fire company.

Chaos erupted. People were yelling, we were getting ourselves and our purses out of the car and trying to unload the horses, who were understandably a bit skittish at all the commotion. Vivian got her horse out right away, but Christi and her dad were having trouble getting full cooperation from a naturally stubborn mare. The fire trucks arrived, sirens screamed, cars stopped, people gawked, and the service station attendant yelled, "It's going to blow up."

Well, it didn't blow up. The fire was soon out. The main problem was that, once again, we were stranded. Our repeated calls for help got us only a busy signal, so we finally had to get an operator to break in on the line at Vivian's house. Her mom was coming to our rescue with a Jeep Cherokee for us to drive. A horse-loving, Good Samaritan stopped, then took Ed to the airport to rent a car for Vivian's mom to drive home. The station closed. It got dark. Traffic slowed. We walked the horses in the grass median strip. We called our insurance agent. We waited. Finally, the Jeep arrived. We loaded up for the third time that day. We were fifty miles from home. Only four hundred to go.

Oops. The connections for the trailer lights didn't match. We couldn't start out with no lights on the trailer. A nearby Kroger store provided the solution. Two flashlights, a pile of batteries, and some heavy tape improvised a primitive system of illumination. It was almost midnight, but we were on our way.

Along toward dawn, Ed fell asleep at the wheel. It seemed only fair—everybody else was asleep! Except the Lord, of course, who, as the Psalm says, "neither slumbers nor sleeps." Thanks to our guardian angels, disaster was averted. Ed woke up when the tires hit the edge of the median strip. So did the rest of us! (He had been driving in the right lane, by the way.) No harm done except a scare sufficient to keep us wide awake the rest of the trip, which was blessedly uneventful.

So you can see why, on the way to the All-Star Game, in someone else's car, on a sunny afternoon, with help on the way, I was content to sit back, relax, pop the top on a Diet Coke, and declare, "This is a great place to have a flat tire."

# fourteen

## Wrapped Up in Red Tape

I still miss Carol. We taught together for a couple of years until she moved away. That was probably fifteen years ago, but I still miss her. She was such a source of encouragement to me. I know what you're thinking. She was one of these bubbly Pollyanna happy-face lookalikes. Wrong. Carol's greeting was usually, "You won't believe what's happened this time!"

This semi-wail of despair/frustration would be followed by a dramatic retelling of her latest head-to-head encounter with bureaucratic obtuseness. (Isn't that a nice euphemism for stupidity?) As long as I knew Carol, she was in a running battle with the telephone company. Along the way, she also grappled with department stores, gas companies, the highway department, and the neighbor's tom cat. Carol is an upbeat, cheerful person, in no way belligerent or quarrelsome—quite the contrary. Still, every day we were treated to a new installment of the Foul-Up Follies.

We all loved it. It made our own frustrations somehow less frustrating. Hey, things could be worse. Carol's adventures made that clear.

Lately, I have begun to think that Carol's mantle has fallen upon me. I would have preferred to be deemed unworthy. I've had quite a variety of my own bureaucratic snafus to deal with, but their range has gradually narrowed. Now my specialty is insurance. When anyone says Blue Cross, I see red. Tape, that is.

If you took all the bureaucrats, tied them up with their own red tape, and laid them end to end... you should just leave them that way.

During a two-year period, every member of our family was hospitalized. The hospitals were in three different states. We were all covered by two group medical plans, both from the same major insurance company. Several acres of trees had to sacrifice their lives to produce the reams of paper consumed in the settling of all the claims involved. This does not include the bills for treatment of backstrain and hernia caused by lifting all those stacks of paperwork. We had to buy a new file cabinet and get the floor reinforced. It would have been cheaper just to pay the medical bills in cash.

Not to mention the phone bills. Of course there is an 800 number. Have you ever tried to call an 800 number? Unless you have automatic redial, which we don't, you'd better have an afternoon to spare, because that's how long it's going to take to get anything besides a busy beep. If you're lucky. Chances are that hunger, nerves, or other physical needs will drive you to give up and call the regular number, suspecting that this is only the first of many calls, the length and frequency of which will substantially bulk up your telephone bill and send quivers of joy through the telephone company stockholders.

Finally, the line is answered. Not by a human being with powers of reasoning, but by a disembodied voice that spits out instructions like a Marine drill sergeant. If this is about a claim, push 4 if it is in-state. Push 5 if it is out-of-state. Push 6 if you are out of your mind. If your name starts with A-M push 1, if N-Z push 2. If you are confused and can't remember your name, push 3. If the final digit of your group number is 0-5, push 7, if 6-9 push 8. Be sure to have ready your policy number, group number, claim number, telephone number, social security number, Visa-card account number and date of expiration, date of service, date of billing, date of birth, date of death, and blood type. If you are still living in the Dark Ages and have a rotary-dial phone, dial 9 and wait for the operator.

I knew there was some reason besides being cheap and old-fashioned for not switching to touch-tone! Now I'll get to talk to a real human being! I gleefully dial 9. Loud soft-rock music.

(How is that possible?) Then a voice with all the personality of a computer hard drive comes on the line: *All of our op-er-a-tors are bu-sy at the mo-ment. Please stay on the line and your call will be an-swered in the or-der it was re-ceived. This is a re-cor-ding.* Thank you for that astounding revelation. I would never have guessed.

More waiting. More ear-splitting music. Then a click. At last, a real person I can talk to. Wrong. It's Mr. All-of-our-operators-are-busy again. Well, I've waited this long. I'll hang in there. More music. If they really wanted you to stay on the line they wouldn't blast that stuff into your ear. But I'll fool them. I'll stick it out. More recordings. More waiting. I dig in and hunker down. It's a mind game now. An endurance test. I refuse to hang up.

"Hello, this is Kevin. How may I help you?" Success! Not necessarily. The chances are very good that Kevin is only one gray cell smarter than Mr. All-our-operators-are-busy. After carefully explaining that certain collection agencies are threatening me with possible incarceration because of unpaid bills for luxuries like ambulances, X-rays, and anesthesia, I can expect one or more of the following to happen:

1. *Absolutely nothing.* Kevin will promise to take care of everything, assure me I have nothing to worry about, and then disappear from the face of the earth.
2. *The X-ray bill will be paid twice, the ambulance not at all.* The mail will continue to bring threatening letters from the collection agency.
3. *Kevin will say that the matter is out of his jurisdiction.* I need to talk to Major Medical. No, he cannot transfer my call. I'll have to call back. But did I know there was an 800 number?
4. *Kevin will look at my account on his computer and declare that everything has already been paid.* Nevertheless, the bills will continue to arrive. I will call back. Since there is no

possibility of ever talking to the same person twice, I spill my guts to Debbie, who pulls up my account on her computer and tells me that the claims have *not* been paid. She will take care of everything. Sure. When pigs fly.

5. *I will call back, speak to yet another person who tells me that the problem is not with my account.* It's the co-insurance. But I was told my insurance was primary because of something explained to me as the birthday rule. Yes, but that's only for myself and the children. I will have to talk to someone who handles my husband's policy. No, he cannot transfer me to that department, but did I know there was an 800 number?

6. *I will write a desperate letter to a local TV consumer protection reporter and within three days get a call from the insurance company.* THEY ARE CALLING ME! IT'S THEIR QUARTER! Finally there will be action. It will still take over a month to get things squared away, but victory is in sight. Oh, yes, I have to send a check for $47.53. I don't ask why. I just mail it in. Willingly.

What really happened? All of the above.

Once I had achieved my consumer-advocate-assisted victory over this monument to bureaucracy, I felt I was home free. There followed many foul-up free months. But just the other day I got a phone call. Just exactly when did I propose to pay my forty-odd dollar department store bill? I would be happy to pay it, I explained, if someone could be bothered to send it to me. They did and I did. But the bills kept coming. Finally, I scrawled STOP SENDING ME THESE BILLS on one and sent it back. This week I received a note of apology from the company president.

Last week Greg called from a motel in another state. His credit card had been denied. Here we go again. We later discovered there was a small unpaid balance for which we had never received a bill. Help! It's starting all over again. A twist here, a twist there, and you're mummified in red tape. I can't take it.

Carol, please move back. I knew I would miss you when you moved away. I just didn't know how much. It never occurred to me that I was the heir apparent to all your bureaucratic woes. We weren't really *that* close, were we?

# fifteen

## What Do You Say to a Naked Fuchsia?

Do you talk to your plants? You're supposed to, you know. It makes them grow better. I don't know exactly what you are supposed to say. Just little pep talks, I guess. Like that frozen vegetable commercial on TV where the little plants in the valley are urged to "GROW FASTER!"

I'm ashamed to admit that I don't have regular conversations with the green and growing things in my house. Unless it's sealed in Tupperware in the back of the refrigerator. Then I just ask for name, rank, and serial number in an effort to make a positive identification so I can decide whether to toss it in the garbage, grind it in the disposal, or bury it in the backyard.

Conversing with plants strikes me as a one-sided effort. But then, most of us women are used to that. The problem is that I'm afraid anything I say would just make matters worse. "Oh, you poor thing" is not exactly an encouraging word.

I did speak to my polka dot plant the other day. It had been doing quite well—I hesitate to say "flourishing"—before we went on a ten-day vacation. I came home to find it dry and withered. What could I say but "You look awful!"?

"You didn't water my plants!" I accused my son.

"Oh, yes, I did," he retorted. "This morning."

Oh, well, it was living on borrowed time, anyway. I'd had it all of six months.

My sordid tale of houseplant homicide began many years ago when my very first homeroom class gave me a tall, lush-leafed philodendron. I brought it home, watered it, bought polish for its big green leaves, fed its roots, trained its little tendrils, and then watched helplessly as it dropped leaf after puny yellow leaf until all that remained was a bare vine, like a green-coated extension cord, wound around a wooden stake.

That was the first indication that my thumbs were as brown as dead pine needles. I've been in denial ever since then, refusing to accept the fact that, for green and flowering plants, my touch is the kiss of death. To the delight of seed companies and nurseries, I keep trying. But I always forget about talking to the plants. Until it's too late.

The years have been marked by numerous casualties: a stunning pink tuberous begonia I got while I was in the hospital that went into a state of decline as soon as I got it home, an asparagus fern that produced enough prickly brown needles to mulch a garden, African violets that bloom profusely and then suddenly and inexplicably shrivel up and expire, blue ageratum that lasts until the original blossom fades (about two weeks) and never recuperates. (I looked that one up in my gardening book to see how to spell it. "Blooms over long period," it said. Sure it does.)

Every year on Mother's Day our church gives out little plants to all the mothers. Every year I kill mine. This year, I was determined things would be different. The little begonia did so nicely for a while that I transplanted it to a larger pot. When I went to water it a couple of days later, it had collapsed. That's the only word to describe it. It didn't turn brown or fall over or anything. It just collapsed into a pathetic blob, like the wicked witch in *The Wizard of Oz*.

For years I had coveted a tall palm tree for my living room. Finally, one Christmas my less-than-subtle hints hit pay dirt and I was presented with a lovely specimen. It was exactly what I wanted. It was brown by New Year's Day.

I thought the jinx had been broken when I discovered the aloe plant. A friend gave me two little starter sprigs. I brought them all the way home from Georgia, and the stuff went wild. It grew out of a succession of ever-larger pots. Those things would grow right up out of the soil, flop over, and demand a new home. I potted and repotted. We had a constant supply of baby aloes. They reproduced and multiplied in biblical proportions and threatened to fill the whole earth with their descendants. I threw them away. I gave them away. But they didn't die. Ever. One Christmas we gave a large party and allowed no one to leave without taking an aloe plant in a baggie tied with a red ribbon. Then, as suddenly as the plagues of Egypt, death descended. They all rotted and returned to the earth whence they came.

I also love ivy. I know lots of people with ivy in their yards. They're always pulling it up and cutting it back. "You can't kill the stuff," they say. I can. I have.

I used to have a Norfolk pine in a large pot that grew over two feet tall. I kept it in my room at school and hung little colored balls on it at Christmastime. The kids called it my Charlie Brown Christmas tree. I had it for several years before it went into terminal droop. We were saddened by its demise.

In spite of all this, I have two spider plants that have lasted longer than it took the macramé holders they were suspended in to rot. I treasure my successes. So you can perhaps understand my antagonism toward the bold and brazen groundhog who was sitting in the window box yesterday, munching on my petunias, which were actually doing quite nicely this year.

My horticultural dream, however, has been to have hanging baskets like the ones I see blooming gracefully and profusely on porches everywhere I go. The problem is that we live on a rather high and windy hilltop. There are days when our cast-iron dinner bell near the back door rings without anyone pulling the rope. Still, wind or no wind, I craved hanging baskets. Mother's Day this year brought wish fulfillment: a lovely fuchsia plant.

May is a bit early for outdoor plants here, so I kept it inside at first, but any place I had to hang it was too dark. The weather took a fine turn, so outside went the fuchsia. Then the weather took another turn. Then another. The poor fuchsia was shuffled in and out, usually ending up at the wrong place at the wrong time. By the time we were able to sit outside and enjoy the flowers, not only had the hot pink blooms all dropped, but the leaves had also perished. Long, bare stems with a few tiny forlorn leaves at the ends were all that survived. All summer, the poor plant hung naked. Then one day I noticed tiny buds. The fuchsia lives! Today it is in full bloom. Unfortunately, there are no leaves, but large, lovely blossoms adorn the ends of spindly, barren stems.

Now what can I say? I'm sorry you look so ridiculous? Would you care for some artificial leaves? A leafpiece, perhaps? Or should it be something consoling (and insincere) like, "Your beauty is only enhanced by the contrast with those bare stems, like a flower in the desert"? Well, what *do* you say to a naked fuchsia?

Christi called the other day.

"Mom," she said, "I think I've killed my cactus."

That's my girl!

# sixteen

## Winter Wonderland

I was ten years old before I saw snow. I will be happy if I don't see any more until I'm a hundred and ten.

We visited friends in Minnesota one summer and I had to ask why all the cars had electric plugs hanging out of the front grills. Hey, I'm from the South. I didn't know some people have to plug their cars in to heaters so they will start in the cold— "cold" being defined as twenty below and lower.

For me, cold starts at sixty. That's *above* zero.

Kathy, who teaches next door to me, is a snow bunny and just loves winter. When we finally got back to school last winter after a week-long blizzard that put our little town on the national news as having the deepest snowfall in the country, she did have the good grace to look apologetic.

"I hope you're happy," I grumbled.

"But it is beautiful," she said.

Well, of course it is. In the woods just below our house, the trees grow tall, their tops meeting across the curving road. After a snowfall, it's a scene of Christmas-card beauty. You wouldn't be at all surprised to meet a sleigh drawn by a team of harness-jingling Clydesdales. A real winter wonderland.

The word "wonder," however, doesn't mean just awe and amazement. It also means to question or puzzle over something, as in "I Wonder Who's Kissing Her Now," or "You'll wonder where the yellow went when you brush your teeth with...." The older I get, the more I find to wonder about.

Here are some of the things I wonder about in the winter:

- Will the next phone call announce a snow day? (And you thought it was just the students who want to know!)

- Will I be able to get my car up the hill?
- If I get up the hill, will I be able to get into the garage?
- How long before the electricity goes off?
- How long before the electricity comes back on?
- Does anyone realize that when country folk lose their electricity they also lose their water? Does anyone care?
- Will the roof leak when the snow melts?
- Will the roof fall in before the snow melts?
- Will I get another chance to play chicken with the big yellow PennDOT snowplow?
- Why does a snowstorm always arrive when the refrigerator is bare, the books are all read, and there's nothing on TV?
- If snow is so great, why did the guy who wrote "White Christmas" live in L.A.?
- Why do I live at this latitude? Why does anybody?

Anyway, it's in the high nineties today. Some folks with short memories are complaining about the heat. Not me. The yard is full of sunshine. The roof is covered with it. So is the sidewalk. And the driveway. And not one bit of it has to be shoveled.

Isn't it wonder-ful?

# seventeen

## Four-footed Beasts and Creeping Things

Picture this: a green pasture surrounded by rolling hills. In the foreground, a stream flows gently. Clover is in bloom, daisies and cornflowers wave in the breeze. Cattle graze placidly in a perfect scene of bucolic peacefulness. Who hasn't driven by such a roadside sight and dreamed of moving to the country?

Before you lose your head and take that giant step, look a little more closely. You will see that at least one of those cows will have its head through the fence, believing the grass to be greener on the other side. It rarely is. Usually the only place the grass is greener is in places where it's heavily fertilized.

Cattle, of course, don't know this; therefore, they are not always inclined to stay in the fields where cows are supposed to be. Pasture, meadow, lawn, garden—it's all the same to them. Over the years, I've had quite a few close encounters with cows—and a few with bulls—but none of them has been of the pleasant kind. I'm not paranoid; it's just that I think they're out to get me. Could there be a sinister side to the herd instinct?

You know how you always see cattle grouped together? Do you know why? I don't have proof, but I have always suspected them of getting together and plotting. I could just hear them saying stuff like "Sunday morning. Nine o'clock. The family will be dressed for church by then. Meet you in the garden." Or maybe "Company's coming for dinner tonight. Six-thirty. Let's all gather in the road in front of the house, say a quarter after." Sorry, Organized Animal Lovers of America, but I'll have to say that it was not a sad day for me when the last Black Angus left on the homeplace was in the freezer.

I was actually able to enjoy a few years of not tensing up when the phone rang, knowing that no one would say, "your cattle are in our garden" or listening for the squeal of brakes as neighbors slowed down to avoid a cattle collision. But then Greg graduated from college and announced his intention to return home and "run a few head of cattle on the farm."

"Run" is the operative word here.

"Listen," I said. "Let's get this straight. Buy all the cows you want. But just remember, they are *your* responsibility. My cow-chasing days are over."

"Fine, Mom. I understand. No problem."

NO PROBLEM until I'm the only one home for the weekend and the neighbor calls to say guess whose cows are in their yard harassing their dog. So then guess who is out in the field in ten-degree weather, trudging through half-frozen mudholes, beating on a grain bucket and yelling "sckow... sckooow"? Of course, one deep ice-crusted hole had to break through, plunging my foot into a thick, black, highly unpleasant substance over the top of my shoes, which are called—appropriately enough—"muckers."

NO PROBLEM until I get home from school and find the calves in the road. It's been a nice day, but the minute I get out of the car, it starts raining. It rains for fifteen or twenty minutes—just until I get those tag-playing calves back in the gate—and then stops. The only time it rained all day.

NO PROBLEM until I'm late for school and semi-frantic and *his* cattle are calmly sauntering down the middle of the road. They never get out in the morning until they know I'm the only one left at home. I could swear they watch until the other vehicles leave. It's some kind of bovine mind game.

You probably always thought cattle were dumb, docile, but ultimately useful creatures. So did I. I never suspected the diabolical schemes they were capable of designing. Well, the scales have fallen from my eyes and I now know a lot more about cows than I ever wanted to know.

Horses, on the other hand, I had always admired as beautiful, classy, intelligent creatures. This impression was purely theoretical, my earliest equine acquaintances being from books and movies: Black Beauty, My Friend Flicka, Trigger. Theory ultimately gave way to experience, and then to disillusionment as I discovered that these beauteous beasts can be a lot more trouble than cattle. The difference is that they aren't being malicious about it. It comes naturally. Horses are just good buddies who like to play games like Follow the Leader. They will sometimes let you be "It"—especially if you are carrying a bucket of oats. This game is much more fun when played in a foot of snow and at distances of more than a mile from home.

Horses are self-possessed, rather pushy creatures who have no qualms about violating your personal space. They bump and nudge you, step on your feet, bite your hair, pull on your clothes, stick their noses in your pockets, and occasionally take a little nip at you if they want more attention or are displeased about something. Horses aren't known for having good eyesight, but our gelding Nub must have thought five-year-old Greg's blond hair looked like hay when he took a mouthful and lifted the poor kid a foot off the ground. Maybe they're just not as smart as they are given credit for being. On the other hand, they can quickly master the art of unlatching stall doors with Houdini-like skill.

I also now know more about horses than I ever wanted to learn. Like how long it takes to rip your fingers raw pulling burrs from a tail. Or the joys of standing on an upturned bucket in a freezing barn at 6 A.M., plaiting the mane of a fidgety mare into thirty-six (count 'em) braids. Or that a runaway horse will stop if you throw your body, arms stretched wide, directly in his path of flight. (Try it sometime.) Or how long it can take to load a mare named Toxic Shock into a trailer when it's not her chosen means of transportation.

One good thing about large animals: even though they aren't always perfectly satisfied with their accommodations, they don't expect to share yours.

We bought our old farmhouse as a single-family dwelling. It has been our intention to keep it that way. It has not been easy. From time to time a number of smaller "beasts of the field" have moved right in and tried to establish squatters' rights. I don't really mind an occasional cricket or even the families of ladybugs that we have been hosting for the past couple of years. I'm talking about creeping and crawling creatures with less savory reputations.

We had been on the farm only a few weeks the first time I discovered that I was not alone. It was fall, and our newly installed furnace was purring away, keeping the house toasty warm in spite of the inevitable old-house drafts. As I swept the dining room I discovered, curled cozily into a sleeping coil next to the hot air register, a snake. It was young, it was small, it was non-poisonous. None of which mattered to me. It was a *snake*. I froze, not daring to move. No that's not right. *Unable* to move. I was afraid of disturbing the unwelcome visitor. The last thing I wanted was that thing slithering around the house. Quickly and quietly I eased out to the kitchen and grabbed an empty mayonnaise jar. As stealthily as the murderer in an Edgar Allan Poe story, I slipped up on the torpid reptile and turned the jar upside down over him. That was all my nerves could stand. There he remained, like a jewel in a museum display, until the master of the house could come home, make merry over the situation, and dispose of the intruder.

Then there was the matter of a somewhat larger version of the same creature who somehow appeared in the bathtub. *Upstairs*. Don't ask how. I have no idea. I found myself unequal to that confrontation. I fled. Fortunately, our indispensable neighbor Jack was at home. Since he had survived an attic-to-basement invasion in his own house of what looks like a copperhead but is really something called an upland house snake, I left the situation in his experienced and capable hands.

On another warm afternoon I decided to sit on the deck and

read the paper. I usually don't even look at the handle of the storm door before I push it open, but this time I happened to glance down and notice that it was already being used. This little guy, not more than a foot long, was balanced, neatly draped in equidistant sections across the latch. As usual, I was alone, and to this day I cannot recall how I handled that one. It must have been traumatic enough to induce selective amnesia, like on the soap operas.

I know these creatures are harmless, but they scare me to death. My response is not rational; it's pure gut emotion. In one of her poems, Emily Dickinson calls that cold feeling of revulsion "zero at the bone." It seems to me that the biblical serpent must have been much more attractive than the snakes I have met for Eve to stay around and chat.

One day I reached up to pick a green apple from the tree across the road and found the stem encircled by a matching green snake—a slender little fellow only a few inches long. He didn't speak to me and believe me, I didn't initiate a conversation. Too bad Eve didn't have the same reaction!

For several blissful summers I saw no snakes. Then last month Greg came in announced the size of a black snake he had just killed. "Where was it?" I asked. "Out in the meadow?"

"Nope."

"Up the road?"

"Nope."

"In the yard?"

"Yep." He grinned. "Heading toward the house."

He got out of the room before the pillow hit him.

When I mentioned this to our neighbors, Barb reminded me of the old saying that "where there's one, there are two." Great. Thank you for sharing that.

A week later, my evening walk was cut short halfway down the sidewalk. I retreated quickly into the house and told Greg to get his shoes on while I got the hoe. "I guess this must have been the other one," he said, after disposing of all four feet of it. "But it was bigger. And closer to the house."

We've had other creatures who have attempted to share bed and board in our home as well. Little guys with beady eyes and long tails who like to move in when the weather turns cool in the fall. Usually a simple trap takes care of these unwanted visitors, but an occasional smart aleck will avoid capture and, emboldened with success, venture among us. While I freeze at the sight of a snake, a mouse has the opposite effect. I scream. I jump up on the furniture. Just like in the comics.

One unlucky little rodent made the mistake of exiting the pantry by way of the den one night when both male members of the household were present. I spotted him first, let out a bloodcurdling yelp and hopped up on the back of the sofa while my heroes gave chase. Greg was armed with a broom, and Ed grabbed the item nearest at hand, which happened to be a cowboy boot. I stayed on top of the sofa.

After the initial shock, I wasn't so scared that I couldn't appreciate the scene that was unfolding before me. Picture it: gray-templed local banker, Rotarian, church and hospital trustee, usually seen in dignified gray suits and conservative wing-tip shoes, now barefoot and in baggy pajamas, brandishing a lethal cowboy boot, in hot pursuit of a terrified little field mouse. Greg would head it off with the broom and Ed would swat at it with the boot. The little fellow was quick enough to ultimately evade the posse, and for some reason we weren't bothered for a long time after that. I think he spread the word: *Steer clear of the big crazy guy with the cowboy boot.* Listen, I would gladly spring for a whole pound of cheddar if I could get that little guy to come back and do it again when I had a loaded camcorder ready. A performance worthy of "America's Funniest Home Videos," and I missed it.

So you want a taste of quiet, peaceful, uneventful country life? Cows in the garden, horses in the road, snakes in the bathtub, mice in the pantry, birds in the fireplace... Oh, didn't I mention the birds?

So you think a chimney sweep is a soot-faced little urchin from *Mary Poppins*? Wrong. It's a bird with long black wings that loves to come down chimneys, cling to the bricks inside your fireplace, and then, when you are innocently eating your lunch, do an unannounced fly-by that sends you and your tuna fish sandwich diving for cover.

Friends were visiting us last week, and somehow the subject of birds in the house came up in the conversation.

"Well," Anita said, "I was sitting in the living room last week and a duck walked by."

"A duck?" I asked.

"A duck. A coal black duck."

I was enchanted. *It wasn't just me!*

Terrill and Anita live in Minnesota, and occasionally a wild duck will make its way down a chimney, just as the swifts do here. This one, in a monument to bad timimg, was unfortunate enough to arrive during a furnace malfunction that covered everything in the house, including stray ducks, with an oily black film.

Well, nobody expects country living to involve drop-in fowl or live-in snakes or fugitive livestock. But truthfully, how often does reality fully measure up to anticipation? Whether it's that dream job, the "made-in-heaven" marriage, long-awaited parenthood, an idyllic summer vacation, or a twentieth (it can't be!) high-school reunion, it's pretty safe to say there will be some surprising turns in the road. Not to mention a few cow patties along the way for the unwary.

Cows aren't the only creatures looking for greener pastures. Haven't you heard teenagers declare, "I can't wait till I'm eighteen. I'm outta here!" A few years later they're back, dragging their stereo systems and thrift-store furniture behind them. Even those who don't return soon find that the exciting, "liberating" experience of being independent is more demanding and less fulfilling than they had imagined.

People don't go into marriage expecting to be divorced, yet half of those who say "I do" end up saying "I don't."

Parenthood turns out to be the most enlightening experience of all. You see kids rebelling and getting in trouble and hear them backtalking their parents and say, "Not my kids." You can have the love of the Prodigal's father, the understanding of Solomon, the patience of Job, and more solid Christian family values than the 1992 Republican Party platform, but that's no guarantee that you're going to be nominated for Mother of the Year.

You hold that little newborn with its sweet-smelling little head (why do babies' heads always smell so good?) and imagine how close you're always going to be. The toddler throws his arms around your legs and cries, "I wuv you, Mommy," and the next thing you know a teenager is slamming a door in your face. A lovable, agreeable, compliant child turns twelve and becomes an obnoxious smart-mouth. Your college student comes home and announces that your perfectly normal family is now considered dysfunctional. Hardly what you expected for twenty-seven hours of labor pains and nineteen years of parenting pains!

Even the Christian life doesn't always work out the way we had anticipated. "It's not like what I expected," a friend said at Bible study one night. It wasn't a complaint—just an observation. Sometimes we have to climb some steep and rocky roads, but that doesn't stop us from stretching our necks toward green pastures and still waters. And when we get there, we realize we're better off for having made the journey. Who wants—or needs—a God who is so small he fits into our puny little schemes and plans? It works a lot better the other way around.

"God created man in his image," Mark Twain said, "and man has returned the compliment." The God we imagine is too often one created out of our own daydreams, wish-lists, and half-understood truths. We've managed to turn him into some sort of celestial Santa Claus, and then we want to climb up into his lap, pull his beard, and coax him into giving us whatever we want.

That's not how it works. I'm glad. Aren't you?

# eighteen

## "Ask the Animals, and They Will Teach You"

People with pets live longer. At least that's what recent studies indicate. Not only do pet people live longer, but they enjoy better health than those who dwell in pet-free zones. Do you have high blood pressure? Depression? If you are stressed out, let a critter into your life.

I must be doing something wrong. My personal relationships with house pets, I must confess, have not had the salubrious effect one might hope for in the light of the scientific evidence. Maybe it's because I was not allowed to have pets as a child. Well, there was one exception. But it took those goldfish such a short time to go belly-up that they really don't count. Things might have been different if we'd had time to bond.

The fact that my father vetoed pets did not prevent his keeping chickens—big, fat, smelly, hateful birds with an attitude. The worst of the foul fowl was an old rooster who would just as soon spur you as peck at his feed. Just take one look at a rooster and you won't need a dictionary to tell you where the word "cocky" comes from.

Now if this were a movie, you know what would happen. The poor little pet-deprived kid would adopt one of those hens and become emotionally attached while she hatched her brood of chicks and then maybe even save the old girl from the stewpot. Nope. It didn't turn out that way. While I didn't relish seeing headless birds flop around after Daddy tied them to the clothesline and decapitated them, I was perfectly willing to douse them in a pot of scalding water and endure the smell while we plucked away those hot wet feathers. It was worth it all when Mama would fry them crispy-brown in her old black iron skillet and I could fight with my brother over who got the pulley-bone. I'm afraid there was no sentiment involved. A chicken was what it was, and that wasn't exactly the sort of cuddly creature I had in mind.

Years later, married and settled in a cozy little duplex apartment, I was finally free to go pet-hunting. We drove off one Saturday morning to a kennel and came back with a brown furry ball that had a tiny plume of tail on one end and enormous chocolate-colored eyes protruding from a flat black face on the other. LuLu the Pekingese was to be with us for twelve years, for better or for worse, and much of it the latter.

That adorable little fuzzball turned out to be the most disagreeable housepet since the first Egyptian let the cat come inside. We spoiled her dreadfully. I blush to remember taking bowls of carefully boned chicken to the doggie hospital during visiting hours when she got sick. There's not a whole lot that will get me to stand over a sink and bone chicken today, and I'm sure not going to do it for a dog. Especially not a dyspeptic, ill-tempered little mutt who terrorized small children and literally bit the hand that fed her, if it belonged to anyone other than the only two people she liked (my husband and me) and the half-dozen she tolerated. She hated men—wouldn't let my brother-in-law in his own house when we went to visit—and never forgave us for having the kids.

"Oh, she's so *cute*," people would say, reaching to pet her. Whereupon LuLu would growl and attempt to amputate a finger. I truly believe I was the only one who mourned her passing.

While our Peke was cute and cuddly, my next dog—a surprise gift from my husband and the kids—was gorgeous and elegant. Kelly, a burnished-copper Irish setter, was a thing of beauty, but unfortunately not a joy forever. She was unquestionably the dumbest dog that ever lived, and the clumsiest. Virtually unteachable, she ran the hills of our farm, free as the wind. She also ran the neighbor's sheep. At least that's how we accounted for the buckshot she wore home in her hind leg one day.

Kelly was thoughtful and generous, bringing the bounty of her hunting—usually a semi-decayed groundhog—and placing it carefully at the back door, where our guests most often enter. Kelly and I would go for long walks—if I could keep her from wrapping herself around my legs and taking me down like an Olympic wrestler pinning the village wimp. This abundant exuberance once leveled me in the middle of a snow-covered road and her playful affection kept me on my back so long that I thought we would surely both be run over.

This brainless beauty insisted on chasing cars in the most reckless manner, and one winter afternoon I thought the school bus had finally done her in. Fortunately, only the long fringes of her coat were caught under the front tires, which pushed her along the icy roadway until the driver finally got stopped and Kelly made her yelping escape. She never learned.

Perhaps a brighter dog would create less anxiety. Enter the Border Collie. This born-and-bred-to-work breed ranks Number One on the Canine I.Q. List. Trixie, I soon learned, was aptly named. She quickly figured out the trick of getting the screen door open and was discovered wolfing down two pounds of hamburger left thawing on the kitchen counter. Later, Trixie II proved to have some tricks or her own: assassinating innocent sheep and attacking the ankles of unsuspecting visitors. Alas, canine crime does not pay, and Trixie had to go.

Just when I had about as much stress-relieving as I could stand, the hunting dogs came on the scene. Sadie Hawkins, a hyperactive beagle pup, would escape and disappear for hours, necessitating high-anxiety moonlight searches across the meadow and through the woods. Then there were the noisy, deep-voiced hounds. If you have never been awakened by a Treeing Walker coon dog baying outside your window in the dead of night, you have missed the most hair-raising, goose-pimpling, sleep-robbing experience of your life.

Maybe I should have taken one of those psychological profiles to see if I was a dog person. Maybe I had the wrong pet. I should get a cat. It's a less demanding relationship.

Cats always did make me a little uneasy. Maybe the memory of a dairy-farming family that attended one of my father's churches had something to do with it. I was just a child, but sort of had the feeling that allowing a dozen or more cats to wander at will between the barn and the house, sipping from pans of milk that were destined to end up in a big tanker truck that afternoon, or, on occasion, dropping unexpectedly from a high perch into the middle of the dining table while a meal was in progress, was not something the Board of Health would look upon with favor. I know I didn't.

Still, I didn't protest when my husband announced, "You've got to have cats on a farm." One day he came home with a little orange-and-white ball and a little gray-and-white-ball. I named them Gertrude and Geraldine. He took those kittens up to the barn and dropped them into a feed barrel with half a dozen mice running around in the bottom. Then he put the lid on. In a few minutes, G and G emerged, and the barrel was empty. It doesn't take long to train a cat.

Since then we've been engaged in an endless battle of wits with a virtual cat dynasty. I think I might win at least an occasional skirmish if cats weren't so quick. A speeding bullet has nothing on a cat that spies a crack in a storm door. They know which one closes fast and which gives them more time. They can set up a maternity ward in a nook or cranny you would swear a cricket couldn't invade. Cats do like to take possession.

If you're having a cookout, a dog will hang around and beg for handouts; a cat will catapult itself into the middle of the picnic table and bury its nose in the veggie dip the minute you turn your back. If you're taking a walk, a dog will follow, but a cat likes to run ahead, then double back and weave in and out of your ankles in a determined effort to send you sprawling face first. Just getting safely to the mailbox and back is a daily challenge of wits and timing.

I never wanted a cat in the first place.

I was pulling weeds out of the marigolds this morning and our yellow tomcat was doing his boa constrictor impression around my feet. I had to nudge him out of the way with my toe every time I took a step. When I put the snippers to a dead blossom, he pushed against my hand, effectively deadheading the plant and saving me the effort of squeezing the handles together. His motor was running all the time, and he seemed quite pleased with his contribution to keeping the marigolds blooming.

We're down to one dog now, and we wouldn't have her if anyone had listened when I kept saying, "You'd better get that beagle to the vet before it's too late." So now we have a half beagle, half shaggy-white-dog-from-the-bottom-of-the-hill, named Disney because she looks like a refugee from a Disney movie. Actually, she's a dead ringer for the footstool/dog in "Beauty and the Beast." She acts like a beagle, though, and runs with that dainty, stiff-legged Beagle gait, and bounces Snoopy-like through the grass. She holds me hostage in the house. I am forced to do several outdoor tasks in one trip because she expects a treat every time the back door opens. Now where in the world would an unwanted, funny-looking, long-haired, off-white, untalented, more or less worthless half-beagle learn a thing like that?

In the midst of all his tribulations Job said, "Ask the animals, and they will teach you." Our animals have taught me that I could be scooting around town in a sporty little red Jag for what they have cost us over the years. As for the amount of time, worry, anxiety, and plain old aggravation—well, if we could put a price on it and Ed McMahon called to say, "You are already a winner," we'd still be in the hole. As for living longer, the stress just could send you with gray hairs to an early grave—unless your children put you there first.

So, fellow pet-fanciers, if Fido or Fluffy has made your life healthier, I congratulate you. If not, welcome to the club. Do you think we should get out of the pet-loop? Cut our losses and bail out of the domestic animal market?

Disney is lying out on the deck in the sunshine, doing the only trick she knows—a totally convincing imitation of a shaggy rug. As I approach, she doesn't open her eyes, but her tail begins to thump against the deck, faster as my steps grow closer. That tail is an amazingly accurate gauge of the proximity of a family member. One word from me, even if it's "mutt," and she jumps up, wriggling ecstatically. She trusts me. She needs me. She's always glad to see me. And she never talks back. I guess I'll keep her.

But that's it. No more. Absolutely not.

Unless, of course, the person who put that For Sale ad in the paper about chocolate Labrador retriever pups happens to return my call....

# part four

## Chuckles and Complaints; Peeves and Pleasures

Who knows the explanation of things? **Ecclesiastes 8:1**

Life is filled with questions. I'm not talking about big questions, like what might have caused a hole in the ozone layer or linguistic puzzles. Like why we park in a driveway and drive on a parkway. Or even why I always get the shopping cart with one whumpyjawed wheel. I've given up asking why, in a store with seventeen checkouts, I invariably get behind the one customer who will need a price check. I guess there are some things we're just not meant to understand. Still, "why?" is usually the first question a child asks... and asks... and asks. Some of us never outgrow it. When we say "Hmmm, wonder why that is," we're not necessarily pondering the deep mysteries of the universe, but simply asking, in an Andy Rooneyish fashion, "Didja ever notice...?"

# nineteen

## Dire Warnings and Signs of the Times

Have you ever lived in the valley of indecision, wanting desperately to rip those "DO NOT REMOVE UNDER PENALTY OF LAW" tags from your sofa throw cushions but afraid the Pillow Police might show up in the dead of night, break your door down with one mighty jackbooted kick, and haul you away to solitary confinement, where you will be forced to iron 100% cotton white dress shirts for the next ninety-nine years? Relax. It won't happen.

Like many new brides, I was terrorized for years by those nasty little tags. They weren't so bad on mattresses because I only saw them when I changed the sheets, or even on bed pillows, if I remembered to stuff that end into the pillowcase first. But there they were on my furniture, constantly popping out and having to be tucked in whenever company was coming. Finally, in a burst of civil disobedience, secure in the protection of the First Amendment and strong enough to have survived being a high-school teacher, Little League mother, and children's camp director, I exercised my inalienable right to freedom and ripped those little suckers right off. Boy, that felt good.

Most of us could manage to get through life feeling reasonably safe if we weren't constantly being bombarded with dire warnings. If you listened to them all, you would starve to death. If you barbecue your food, you'll get cancer; if you fry it, you'll have a stroke; if you boil it, you'll lose all the nutrients; if you get desperate and eat it raw, you'll get trichinosis. If you eat fruits and vegetables, you'll be poisoned by pesticides; if you eat meat, you'll be poisoned by growth hormones and other chemicals; if you eat seafood, you'll be poisoned by mercury. And for goodness' sake, don't drink the water. Anywhere. It's contaminated. So is the milk. And the orange juice. Don't even think about sweetening your cereal or coffee in the morning—sugar will kill you just as fast as those artificial sweeteners can eat your brain cells.

Talk about a no-win situation. You have to eat, but if you pay attention to the reports in the media, you could climb to the top of the food pyramid and back down again and not find anything that is safe for human consumption. The inevitable result of this dilemma is massive, widespread anxiety. The kind that can only be relieved by the most comforting of all human activities: eating. Some warnings, however, aren't so frightening. They're just plain insulting. Like this notice on a window air conditioner: MAINTAIN A FIRM GRIP ON AIR CONDITIONER WHEN INSTALLING OR REMOVING. DO NOT ALLOW UNIT TO FALL OUT OF THE WINDOW. Thank you for sharing that bit of advice. It never occurred to me that this thing might fall if I didn't hold on to it. I thought the law of gravity didn't apply to air conditioners.

Reading the instruction book that came with my new Chevy, I ran across this gem of wisdom: HEATER OPERATES MOST EFFICIENTLY IF WINDOWS ARE CLOSED. What a concept! I wonder if that would work at home, too. Maybe next winter I'll try closing the windows when the furnace comes on.

How about those little charcoal nuggets in cereal boxes? DO NOT INGEST. I wasn't planning to. And maybe I won't eat them either.

Speaking of insulting, what really ticks me off are all these symbols that have replaced signs and instructions written in plain English. I can understand Mr. Yuk's picture for little kids who can't read, but surely someone in the car can decipher "McDonald's" instead of relying on those knives and spoons on the interstate signs—which is actually a bit misleading anyway, since we hardly ever see an eating utensil in a roadside restaurant any more.

"Motel" is not a difficult word. Surely it is as recognizable as a half-circle and a dot on top of a rectangle, which I assume is supposed to represent a person lying on a bed. All these signs and symbols are not only frustrating; they're dangerous. I nearly wrecked my son's new pickup truck driving to school one cold morning. I couldn't watch the road and figure out what all those squiggly lines meant. Nothing said "heat" or "fan." Which—had I been able to find—I would of course have operated with the windows down, had it not been for that helpful little booklet prepared by GM.

Then there's that big red circle with the X through it on my hair dryer. I assume that means that it probably would not be good judgment on my part to try to dry my hair while I'm taking a shower. Thanks. I needed to know that.

What about those envelopes that say "Place postage here. Post Office will not deliver unless postage is attached." I didn't know that! All these years I thought the U.S. Postal Service was a charitable organization. You mean we *pay* them to lose our mail?

Be honest now. You've settled back in your La-Z-Boy with your palm-oil-free popcorn to watch a rented video. Doesn't your heart beat just a little bit faster when that FBI notice flashes on the screen at the beginning of the movie? Can't you just imagine the Feds bursting in right in the middle of "Free Willy" to see if you're set up to PLAY and RECORD? It could be the effect of those bold black-and-white graphics, but I haven't got the nerve to defy that one. Shoot, I'm afraid not to *rewind*. Maybe if there were any movies around that were worth watching a second time, I might be tempted.

On the other hand, there are times when a warning would be in order. Even appreciated. Like the time my friend Heather was housesitting and decided to clean the bathroom. The product she used should have carried a warning that said, "If you mix this cleaner with any other chemical it will turn your bathtub bright orange." But it didn't. And it did.

I made a recent purchase that should also have had a warning. One that read like this: If you buy these socks, you will spend five minutes and break three fingernails trying to remove the label that encircles them and which was applied with crazy glue. Then you will need a razor-sharp blade of surgical steel to cut through the half-dozen strips of tough, stringy plastic that hold the pairs together. That mission accomplished, you are left with only the necessity of removing the cardboard forms over which the socks are stretched as tight as the parchment on a bass drum. All in all, this is quite a buy: ten minutes to complete the purchase, fifteen minutes to earn the money, and an hour and a half to unpackage for wearing. You might as well learn to knit.

Although we appreciate the concern for children's safety which prompted the development of the child-proof cap, it would have been nice to indicate an interest in adult safety by attaching a warning which said: IT IS QUITE POSSIBLE THAT YOU MIGHT HAVE A STRESS-INDUCED STROKE WHILE TRYING TO OPEN THIS BOTTLE. I think my sister must have come close when she was driven by a splitting headache to attack an aspirin bottle with a crowbar. She won. In the process she lost all the pills except two, but that was all she needed.

There is a perverse streak in human nature that urges us to ignore warnings. Can you pass a "Wet Paint" sign without giving it just a quick touch? Remember those old computer cards? Weren't you just dying to fold, spindle, or mutilate one? We blithely turn a deaf ear to the voices that urge us to exercise, floss, pre-plan our funeral, eat fiber, and buckle up.

Nowhere is this tendency to ignore warnings more evident than out on the open road. The rare drivers who heed the posted speed limit are generally considered a menace on the highways. Especially since they're always in the fast lane. Most of us give ourselves a few miles leeway, and we still get our doors blown off. I was riding the other day with my friend

Stephanie (not known for her light foot), and we were passed by a kid who was apparently practicing for his pilot's license. In the back window of his sporty little black car was a sign: "Don't look. It's an Eclipse." A few miles down the road, we easily passed the Eclipse. It was standing still. On the side of the road. With a state trooper leaning on the front door. I guess he must have ignored the warning and looked.

Well, Eve started it. She was a great one for ignoring warnings, and look where it got us. Adam too. He didn't listen a bit better than she did. Neither did Lot's wife when she looked back with longing to Sodom. (Which reminds me of the Sunday School teacher who was telling her first graders that Lot's wife looked back and turned into a pillar of salt. "That's nothing," said Johnny. "My mother was driving and she looked back and turned into a telephone pole!")

The Old Testament is filled with stories of people who ignored warnings to their own destruction: the Egyptian Pharaoh who brought down the plagues; Saul, who disobeyed, consulted a witch, and lost his kingdom; Samson, who lost his strength and finally his life; and Solomon, who had everything and forfeited a dynasty.

Sometimes the warnings were not as obvious. I doubt if there was a sign at the harbor in Joppa that said "Not responsible for runaway prophets who board this ship without diving equipment," but it probably wouldn't have made any difference to Jonah anyway.

The parables of Jesus were filled with warnings: the rich fool who was punished for his materialism and selfishness; the foolish virgins, whose carelessness shut them out of the wedding feast; the foolish man who built his house on the sand and saw it destroyed. Jesus knew his listeners well enough to know most of them wouldn't pay attention. If you've got ears, he warned, you'd better listen. We're not very different.

No wonder our kids ignore the constant dire warnings we throw at them. "If you keep crossing your eyes, they'll get stuck that way," or "Your face is going to freeze like that." Then we give them a legitimate warning like "Don't stick your tongue on the ice cube tray," and they don't pay any attention. Sometimes, the less said the better. I've never figured out why my mother told my sister not to put the peas they were shelling up her nose, but she did. And you can guess what my sister did.

We are subjected to so many warnings—foolish, confusing, or unnecessary—that we tend to ignore, challenge, or even defy those which are genuine. Stop. Slow. Yield. Beware. Listen. And here's one that turns up on road signs and is always good for a laugh: Repent.

Like it or not, warnings are there for our good. We ignore them at our own peril.

Don't say I didn't warn you.

# twenty

## The Awful Truth
## or
## What People Won't Tell You

"Any questions?" I closed *Exploring Life through Literature* and looked around the room at the sea of sophomore faces. Amy's hand shot up.

"Mrs. Stiles, did you know you have only one earring on?"

I clapped my hand over my ears, distracted for the moment from Shakespeare's mastery of iambic pentameter. Sure enough, one earring was missing.

"Thank you for telling me, Amy. I must have left it by the telephone." But that was second period and it's lunchtime now! *Why didn't somebody tell me sooner?*

To tell or not to tell? That is the question. It gets asked a lot in advice columns. "Do I tell her, do I not tell her, or do I tell him I'm going to tell her if he doesn't tell her first?" Or "Did you know I saw your fiancé on 'America's Most Wanted' last week?" Of course, that's pretty heavy stuff compared with the daily decisions we have to make, such as whether you should just walk up to someone and say, "Did you know you have a poppy seed stuck between your front teeth?" What about mascara smeared so you look like the Lone Ranger's twin sister? Am I my brother's keeper when he's headed for the choir loft with powdered sugar from the Sunday school class doughnuts delicately dusting the tip of his nose?

The responsibility of enlightening people about something of which they are unaware requires both wisdom and tact. Maybe they would rather not know, preferring blissful ignorance to painful disclosure. That's the risk you take. Most women are inclined to take this very seriously where members of their families are concerned. Especially when it's a husband. It's like they promised to love, honor, obey (or not), and spare from embarrassment so long as they both shall live.

One pastor's wife devoted herself to keeping that vow, and to that end she always sat in the front row at church. Over the years she developed a set of signals as complicated as an NFL referee's to keep hubby posted on how he was doing. One Sunday she tried frantically to catch his eye. Zzzt! Zzzt! she hissed softly, jerking her head sharply backward with each exhalation. Zzzt! Zzzt! Her husband finished the announcements and moved toward his pulpit chair. Zzzt! Zzzt! The upward head-jerking increased, threatening to send the good woman's hat flying into the pew behind her. Zzzt! Zzzt! Zzzt! Suddenly comprehending his wife's distress, the pastor's face turned a deep liturgical red and he hopped back behind the pulpit to once again welcome the visitors. Finally, he took his seat, this time with his fly closed and the offending zipper firmly locked in place.

But not all of us have someone so firmly committed to keeping us from looking foolish. How many times have you stood behind a fellow parishioner, trying to concentrate on the Apostle's Creed, when you're really itching to tuck in a protruding label, button the back of a gaping blouse, or—worse yet—give a tug to a hiked-up skirt? Would it be wrong just to touch the hem of a garment?

How many women have been seated in front of you, meticulously groomed and perfectly coiffed—except for a gap where the crown hair doesn't blend into the back of the head. A couple of brush strokes would have taken care of that. Don't these people look at each other before they leave home? Or at least while they're in the car? From his vantage point in the back seat, it was our son's responsibility to attend to dad's cowlick as he drove to Sunday school, although I would have preferred that he not pretend to spit in his hand before smoothing down Dad's hair. Every family needs a hair patrolperson. I mean, what's a family for?

I just wish someone had been looking the night I left in a rush for a baby shower wearing two different shoes: one black, one blue. Fortunately, it was an informal group who liked to kick their shoes off. I got rid of mine as soon as I walked into the room. When time came to leave, I pulled them out from under the couch, tucked them under my arm, slipped them on at the from door, and made my escape.

Sometimes it may be possible to alleviate a potentially embarrassing situation without letting the other person know. This is especially important if that person is a stranger. Suppose you see someone leave a public restroom with a toilet paper streamer trailing from one shoe. You could just mosey up behind and step on it yourself. Just be sure you don't walk away with it stuck to your own foot. Of course, if the streamer is rather short, you could put yourself in a *really* embarrassing situation. People—especially strangers—tend to be rather sensitive about a violation of their personal space. But if it's a long flyer, be a good Samaritan and take your chances.

My friend Sara chose *not* to tell one day when she stopped at a petting zoo in a shopping mall. Next to her stood a woman and her young grandson. Engrossed in watching the little boy, the woman was oblivious to the baby goat that was methodically chewing away at her skirt.

"Didn't you tell her?" I asked my friend.

"No," she laughed, "I wanted to watch!"

The goat had nibbled its way almost to her waist before the startled lady took notice and began swatting at the innocently offending little creature and shrieking "Get away! Get away!"

The same sort of humiliation would have been mine on another occasion, had I not been fortunate enough to have a loyal colleague come to my rescue when I waltzed from the rest room into the teacher's lounge one lunch period. Just about the time I felt an unusual breeze, Debbie threw herself between me and the other occupants of the room while I quickly dislodged the bottom of my full skirt from the waistband of my panty hose.

I've often wondered what would have happened had I not been among friends. What if I had walked out into the hall instead of into the lounge? No one would have said a word—then. But I can just hear generations of students, for years to come, saying, "Did you ever hear about the time that Mrs. Stiles..." In the high school world, this is the stuff of legends. Personally, I would prefer to sink into oblivion.

I haven't done my research on this, so I don't know what Emily Post or Miss Manners might say, but surely there are some common-sense considerations in situations such as this. How well do you know this person? You might not want to walk up to a total stranger and say, "Did you know you have something green stuck to your tooth?" A roommate from college days told me that during a recent visit her sister said, "Stand up straight. I don't want you to get round-shouldered. And only your sister would tell you that." Another consideration should be the circumstances. I practically had to sit on my hands a few Sundays ago to keep from reaching out to the pew in front of me and tucking in the label on a young mother's dress. But her attention was on her baby, it was quiet in church, and my hands would have been pretty cold on the back of her neck. I decided not to risk it.

One reason to keep your mouth shut could be simply that there is nothing to be done. If someone shows up at a meeting in a blouse adorned with coffee dribbles or returns from lunch wearing gravy on his tie, what is to be gained by making them aware of a problem that can't be solved short of dousing oneself with water in the rest room or removing the offending clothing? However, if the problem is unmatched socks (or shoes!) a friendly tip could permit the person to spend the next few hours trying to stick his feet under whatever piece of furniture might be handy.

"Pardon, your slip is showing" is, of course, the classic but virtually obsolete warning. You hardly ever see a woman with her slip showing any more. Why is this? Don't people wear slips any more? Are hemlines so erratic that slips have been abandoned as a lost cause? Unless, of course, they are being worn *as* a dress rather than *under* a dress.

What do you do about the really personal stuff—dandruff, halitosis, or B.O.? Hey, the path of life is fraught (isn't that a great word?) with hard choices. Moral dilemma is the hallmark of modern life. Let your conscience be your guide. Personally, I never turn down a Certs.

So much for unsolicited intervention. But what do you do when someone actually asks for your opinion? BEWARE! "How do you like my new red dress?" is a loaded question if there ever was one. The answer is not, "It doesn't make you look as fat as the blue one."

When new parents ask, "What do you think of our little Hortense? Isn't she beautiful?" you are tiptoeing through a minefield. Assuming that the proud parents are prejudiced in the child's favor and that you aren't a liar, the best thing to do is fall back on the wise old preacher's safety net and say, "My, oh my, that is *some* baby!"

In some extremely ticklish situations you may be willing to speak up but find it unnecessary. No lady I know who has wandered accidentally into the men's room has waited to be told of her error before she's outta there. Visiting a neighborhood church, my friend Sara (the baby-goat observer, who has a knack for getting into interesting situations) reacted a little slowly when the preacher said, "Bow your heads and close your eyes." Consequently, she was the only one to notice that when the man in front of her stood up, his pants didn't. (It seems the gentleman had recently lost a lot of weight.) There he stood in his union suit. Fortunately, the poor man also noticed something amiss. Unfortunately, when he bent over to pull up his pants, his trap door fell open!

Well, he caught on to that pretty fast, too. So it wasn't necessary for her to tap him on the shoulder and say, "Excuse me, sir, are you aware that you just mooned half the congregation?"

It really wasn't that bad, though. Most of them had their eyes closed, innocently and sincerely singing, "Just As I Am."

# twenty-one

## The Mauving of America

Where were you when President Kennedy was shot? Assuming you are old enough to remember 1963, I'll bet you remember exactly where you were and what you were doing when you heard the news. Images of momentous events—the Challenger disaster, the start of the Gulf War, the already-legendary white Bronco chase—are traced on our memories with indelible ink. They don't dim with the passing of years, even while the routine events of last month or last week are rapidly burrowing deeply into the convolutions of the little gray brain cells, never to see the light of day.

So where were you when America suddenly turned mauve? Betcha can't remember. Neither can I. All I know is that I looked around one day and found myself in a purplish-pinkish haze that has lasted nearly a decade and is just now fading away. Carpets were mauve. Furniture was mauve. Kitchen counters were mauve. Curtains, bedspreads, patio furniture—all mauve. Everything from dish towels to minivans. One of the most amazing phenomena of modern society, and historians will be at a loss as to how to explain it. Since the Mauve Movement occurred on the waning edge of the Geese Period in Modern Decor, some of those omnipresent fowl were actually painted with mauve bills and mauve webbed feet (alert *National Geographic*!) by some enterprising designers eager to jump on (and cash in on) both bandwagons.

Our congregation just happened to be building a new church at the time the Mauve Movement was gaining headway, and we had exactly two color choices for carpet and pew pads: green and—you guessed it—MAUVE. It can only be attributed to divine guidance that we chose green. I know of a church in another state which recently built a megabucks building, ostensibly because the church was enjoying so much growth. I think the real reason was to get away from the old sanctuary, which was decorated in you-know-what-color.

While all this mauving was occurring, I was innocently and blissfully living in my earth-colored world of burnt orange and brown, olive green and gold. As a matter of fact, I am currently awaiting delivery of a new stove—almond in color—to replace my old green one, circa 1971. I'm getting with it, at last. At least I thought so—until I started noticing the new trend in colors. Earth tones.

I was bemoaning my Bicentennial bedroom (circa 1976) the other day to a friend. "It's got red shag carpet!" I admitted in some embarrassment.

"Our bedroom has orange shag," my friend replied. Oops. While I was trying to pry my foot out of my mouth, she added, "It was there when we moved in."

I can't help it. I'm always behind the trends. When I needed true red towels for the bathroom, everything was cranberry. When I needed royal blue for the bedroom, everything was country blue and, of course, mauve. Now the stores and catalogs are full of guess what? Bright red and royal blue! My living room was white and gold when everybody else had soft pastels.

I ordered some new bedroom carpet this weekend, and I was carefully explaining which carpet went in which room. "This one replaces the red shag," I said to the salesclerk, pretending not to notice the smirk she found hard to repress.

What color is replacing my red-white-and-blue? Teal.

OK, so maybe I did decide to go with the flow of fashion for once. Besides, I happen to *like* teal. Whatever color it is. Everything from seafoam to deep blue-green is called teal these days.

In response to the taste of the moment, we have turned our homes into menageries of ducks, geese, pigs, cows, velvet-clad bunny rabbits... and teddy bears in Victorian finery.

Remember those macramé owls that had to come down to make room for Sunbonnet Sue in calico hat and apron? And who would ever have predicted that the ugly duckling of the floral world would blossom into a Sunflower swan?

Who engineers all this? How? I don't know. But whenever the bandwagon comes down the pike, we all jump on.

I will confess to riding the craft bandwagon through the candlemaking and decoupage and crewel embroidery crazes, but I jumped off when we got to quilting. I refinished furniture and antiqued everything that couldn't escape my glaze. But then whose closets couldn't yield an unfinished project or two?

According to the fashion of the day, our yards have been filled with everything from shiny bright-colored "lawn balls" on concrete pedestals to pink flamingoes. Even our cars get in on the act, with "Baby on Board" signs and all the inevitable spin-offs dangling in the back window. Need I mention hula hoops, pet rocks, and mood rings?

Yes, I will admit to occasionally getting caught up in current clothing fads. You never wore bell bottoms? Wire-rimmed glasses whether you needed them or not? Granny dresses and platform soles? If one didn't trip you up, the other would. Too young for that stuff? Then what about big hair, big sweaters, and ripped jeans? You're from an earlier generation? How about saddle oxfords and poodle skirts and pony tails? I can remember girls from my high school riding to the prom in the back seat of the car—alone—because their crinoline petticoats wouldn't fit in the front. The guys didn't like it, but I'll bet the parents did!

I'm not too proud to admit that I used to go to the beauty shop once a week (ugh!) and have my hair abused into a beehive which I wrapped in toilet paper and a nylon net bonnet at night. Hey, it was better than those pink plastic brush rollers, which could only have been created by a man inspired by The Rack and other medieval instruments of torture. I knew girls who slept with their hair wrapped around frozen orange juice cans—not to mention the ones who went to the other extreme in the "natural" seventies and, Cher-like, ironed their long tresses straight.

When I was in high school I can remember very well going into Baker's Shoes at Five Points in downtown Atlanta and saying, "Don't show me any pointed toes." I can also remember going into the same store a year later and saying, "Don't you have anything more pointed?"

Why on earth do we do it?

I don't know. It always seems like the thing to do at the time.

"Monkey see, monkey do," my mother used to say. Which is, I suppose, what the Psych 101 textbooks would also say about the reason we feel compelled to latch on to one fad after another. More often than not, they're harmless. Sometimes they may be silly, like the goldfish swallowing and flagpole sitting of the 1920s. They could even be dangerous. Like bungee jumping.

It happens in religion, too. A few years ago, *The Exorcist* made demon possession a national fascination, and it wasn't long until demons were being cast out of people all over America in every sort of church from great cathedrals to country chapels. You don't hear much about exorcism now, but Frank Peretti's spine-tingling, hair-raising page-turners helped to make spiritual warfare a hot topic and usher in the current age of "angelmania." (I did not make that word up.) When you mix all this with a plethora of near-death, out-of-body experiences, you've got some pretty heady stuff. It's dramatic and a lot more exciting than the Beatitudes or the Golden Rule. And when there's enough truth to mask whatever error might slip in, it's easy for confusion to set in. "Test the spirits," the Bible says. Good advice. No, not just good—vital.

There's not anything wrong with fads in themselves. Fads can be fun. Most are perfectly harmless. You could paint your house chartreuse and wear polyester Nehru jackets till the

Second Coming and the Lord wouldn't mind a bit. But always looking for a new kick could also be the symptom of discontentment. When it comes to fads of the faith, beware.

The Old Testament Israelites wanted a king in the worst sort of way. "We want to be like the other nations," they whined.

"They haven't rejected you," God told Samuel, who understandably got his feelings hurt when they ignored his anti-king warnings. "They have rejected me." Then God let them have their way, but it didn't exactly work out as well as they had anticipated. They followed the crowd right into idolatry. And finally, into captivity.

Not much danger of that these days. Or is there?

# twenty-two

## Prayer and the Information Superhighway

Where do you get your news? Maybe you slip the *National Enquirer* into your shopping cart at the supermarket. Maybe you read *People* at the dentist's office or watch "A Current Affair." If that's not your style, you may prefer Tom or Dan or Barbara or Peter on the networks. You could rely on your local newspaper or favorite radio station. But if you really want to know what's going on in *your* world, I have discovered—quite by accident—the on-ramp to the local information highway. It's found in the Children's Department at your neighborhood church. If you don't believe me, just offer to teach Sunday school or help in children's church. Then ask for prayer requests.

"OK, boys and girls, it's prayer time. Does anyone have any special requests?" Hands wave all over the room, but one little guy just can't wait to voice his concern.

"Pray for my mother," he blurts out. "She's going to have a baby. She forgot to take her pill!"

Apparently she also forgot to inform the child of the difference between public and private petition. But then, some adults have never learned that either, judging from the length and detail deemed necessary to keep the Lord informed of the news of the day and to give him instructions on what to do about it.

Children take prayer very seriously. "Ask, and you will receive," we teach them. So they ask—about whatever happens to be uppermost in their minds at the moment. Medical problems, of course, top the list. Fortunately, children lack the knowledge of anatomy and physiology—as well as the vocabulary—that can turn simple requests into full-blown "organ recitals," as adults are prone to do. Usually a child expresses concern for someone with chicken pox, the flu, or perhaps a bad case of "road rash" from a bike accident. Occasionally, however, it's a public health announcement: "My brother got lice at school."

Sometimes the information highway takes you in a direction you didn't anticipate. During a conversation at a Sunday school class party, I just casually—and quite innocently—remarked that I loved working with kids and had accidentally discovered that it was also a way to learn what's going on. Two ladies responded—too quickly.

"Is something going on?" asked Lady Number One.

"*I* didn't know anything was going on," replied her friend.

Oops. Had I unwittingly hit a nerve? Clearly, something was Going On. But all I *meant* was that I knew whose Grandma had all her teeth pulled and was getting new ones, and whose little brother fell over the cat—which wasn't supposed to be in the house—and had to get sixteen stitches in his head, and who was going to get a new baby brother or sister but his mother didn't want anybody to know yet. This is not the sort of thing you read in the church newsletter or Sunday bulletin.

"I *never* know what's going on," sniffed the first lady.

Sure. And the Pope's a Southern Baptist.

Suddenly I remembered that both ladies had been the objects of their children's prayer requests the previous Sunday. Just exactly how do you pray for somebody who runs a stop sign and wrecks her husband's brand-new, cherry-red sports car? There probably were other petitions we could have sent heavenward in her behalf, but we settled for being thankful no one was hurt.

The other lady would not have been blessed to hear her young son giving a detailed account of a particularly troublesome problem they had been having with rodents—and we're not talking field mice, either. I'm still not sure how I got from Junior's graphic reenactment of the family dog's encounter with these industrial-size invaders to the Throne of Grace, but you'd better believe I got there in a hurry.

I don't claim to have the gift of discernment, but I decided it was time to extricate myself from that conversation and go in search of the veggie dip.

The next Sunday, after musically exhausting all the ways Moses could conceivably have crossed the Red Sea, it was once again time for prayer.

"What are some things we should pray about, children?"

"Pray I won't get an *F* in math!" This response—so specific and so heartfelt—was clearly an urgent need.

A mini-lecture on how we can *help* the Lord answer our prayers seemed to be in order at this point. "Yes, we should ask the Lord to help us with our schoolwork." Then I asked, "Anything else?"

The same little girl's hand shot up. "Pray I won't get an *F* in spelling!"

"OK, Amanda. David?"

Amanda continued to wave her arm while the other children voiced their concerns. Finally, I sighed, "Yes, Amanda?"

"Pray I won't get an *F* in reading!"

I think it would be safe to assume that at least one car in the church parking lot won't be sporting a "My-Child-Is-An-Honor-Roll-Student" bumper sticker.

Then there was the Sunday one little fellow decided to skip the middle man and take his petition to the altar himself. It was during a revival, and the children had joined the adults in the sanctuary. At the close of the service, several went forward. After a few minutes this youngster, who had been crying and praying earnestly, was approached by the visiting minister.

"What are we talking to the Lord about today, son?" he asked.

"Well," the sincere little chap replied loudly, "I've been saying (expletive deleted) a lot lately, and I...."

The red-faced evangelist beat a hasty retreat. The rest of the congregation retreated behind their hankies and Kleenex.

Don't ask a child anything unless you want him to tell you.

Most of the children's requests are predictable: lost puppies, broken bones, dead goldfish. But even when it's lost jobs, broken homes, or a tragic death in the family, the quality of their simple faith remains the same: open, honest, totally trusting.

And it was in that very simplicity of faith that little Molly put her hand up one Sunday and said quietly, "Will you pray for my aunt?"

"Of course, dear. Is she sick?"

"No," Molly replied. "A monkey bit her ear off."

Let us pray.

# twenty-three

## The Call of the Waves
## or
## How I Spent My Summer Vacation

We just got home from the beach last night. My car is full of sand. So are my shoes. Loads of sand-encrusted laundry, smelling of seawater and suntan lotion, are testing the limits of the filtering systems in the washer and dryer even as I write. My sunburn has reached the exquisitely itchy stage, compelling me to periodically wander into the family room and rub my back against the corner of the brick wall, like a hog scratching itself on a fence rail.

Actually, I did much better avoiding sunburn this year. Not once did I find it necessary to sit in a restaurant and slide ice cubes from my water glass down my burning back, as I have been driven to do in the past. That was the summer I went around for days in a white haze of anti-itch medicated powder, looking like a bleached-out version of Pigpen in *Peanuts*. I carried the stuff everywhere with me, giving the term "powder room" a whole new meaning.

Between back-scratchings and the laundry, I unpack groceries that we hauled six hundred miles, unloaded, re-packed, and hauled home again. Good intentions aside, we ate out more than we ate in. And in spite of my determination to turn a blind eye to the seashells littering the shore, a plastic bag of the best of this year's crop will undoubtedly end up in the basement with the as-yet-unopened bag I dragged home last year.

Why do we do this every year?

We do it so we can sit in backed-up beach traffic for that last thirty miles, moving slower than a turtle wearing ankle weights, in 100-degree weather, running the air conditioning and hoping the radiator doesn't overheat and go into its Old Faithful act.

We do it so we can stumble down to the beach every morning, dragging along enough paraphernalia for newlyweds to set up housekeeping. I realized we were traveling light when one guy showed up every day with a full-sized spade and hoe—real garden tools—which he used to put up one small beach umbrella. We're talking major excavation here. I was waiting for him to dump in a bag of concrete. The umbrella, once professionally installed, provided a circle of shade about the size of a sand dollar. Then this guy proceeded to dig a moat for a sand castle that was deep enough to lose a small child in.

People bring *everything* to the beach. As soon as you get it all set up, of course, you have to snatch up your towels and books and ice chest and boom-box and all the rest and move back a few feet to escape the encroaching waves. The tide has no respect for squatter's rights.

Once finally established, the confirmed beachgoer spends the rest of the day seeking out various forms of physical discomfort. Water so cold you turn blue. Waves that knock you down face-first and roll you over until you come up sputtering with a snootful of salt water. Sun that scorches your flesh and sends you back into the frigid brine for temporary relief. Sand inside your bathing suit and between your fingers. Suntan potions that leave your skin so slippery you can't pop the top on a Dr. Pepper can. Wet sand too hard to lie on and soft, dry sand that blows in your face. Webbed aluminum furniture that creases your back and gouges your legs. Sweat down your back and grit in your lemonade.

For this you tried on bathing suits under fluorescent lights in front of a three-way mirror?

All of this we endure so we can spend our hard-earned vacation time in the company of boom-box players, sand kickers, frisbee throwers, jellyfish, and—shades of *Jaws*—sharks. You've never spotted a fin? Neither had I until my personal Close Encounter of the Toothy Kind. I was standing knee-deep in the surf when suddenly something whacked me on the side of my leg. Needless to say, I screamed and quickly sought the shore. Was it really a shark? I refused to believe it at first, but Ed finally confessed that he had seen it. He didn't actually say it was a shark, just that it was about two feet long, gray on top and white on the bottom, and it was smiling!

The next day I had a large bruise on my calf. To satisfy my curiosity, I spoke to the lifeguard.

"I want to ask you something," I said. "Are there any sharks around here?"

"Not *today*," he answered.

We spent the rest of the week at the pool.

Still, we can't stay away from the shore. The sea calls us back, year after year, although I'm a bit more wary now of what might lurk beneath that vast ever-changing surface. Sitting lazily on the beach one afternoon, watching the tide roll in, I began to speculate—aloud—about that long ago day when the first person wandered out of the forest and saw the ocean for the first time. It had to have been an awesome, overwhelming experience.

"I don't know," my sister said. "If the first creatures really crawled out of the ocean, it would have been a familiar sight."

"Couldn't have happened that way," I replied. "Anything that came crawling out on this beach wouldn't have lasted long enough to evolve into anything else. It would have been flattened out of existence before it wiggled halfway across Ocean Drive."

Eureka! We had found it. The flaw in the theory of evolution. The Road Kill Factor. So much for Darwin.

How could anybody sit on the shore and not believe in the God of creation? Forget the colors of the sky, the majesty of the ocean, the constancy of the tides. Look at the people!

Where could such an astonishing assortment of humanity have come from, except from a great Creator with a great heart of love—and a great sense of humor.

A couple of summers ago we were people-watching on the beach when a small group descending the wooden access steps caught our attention. They were definitely overdressed. Or so we thought, until they gathered in a semicircle around a middle-aged woman (judge? minister? justice of the peace?) with a little black book in her hand. A wedding! A sizeable number of uninvited guests watched from a respectful distance and joined in the applause when the groom kissed the bride. The wedding party went their way and we all went back to slathering on sunscreen or reading our mindless beach books or slowly hand-dribbling a tower atop a sand castle, just as if beach wedding parties were as common as seagulls.

Late in the day, the beach is deserted except for a couple of seemingly tireless surfers and a few kite-flyers. We sit and watch our shadows lengthen across the sand or stroll barefoot, wading through the warm shallow tidal pools. Tensions and worries float away like lazy puffs of white clouds drifting out to sea. The world beyond the dunes, for the moment, doesn't exist.

Why do we do this every year? I think I just answered my own question. We do it because it's worth the trouble.

Why would a fisherman go out before daylight and stand in a freezing stream for hours just to have his spot when the season opens? Because to him, it's worth it.

Why do so many people drive themselves to frustration knocking the daylights out of a little white ball that consistently refuses to land anywhere near the spot the golfer had in mind? For some reason that totally escapes me but my husband understands perfectly, it's worth it.

A serious athlete pumps iron and drinks Gatorade while his friends hang out and swill high-test Mountain Dew. A student studies in the library while her friends power-shop at the mall.

A graduate forgoes a steady job and a new car for college dorm life and lectures. A young couple undertakes the endless responsibility and astronomical expense of raising children when just the two of them could afford to drive a sports car, buy a boat, and vacation in the Bahamas. Why? When the rewards so far outweigh the cost, who's even going to ask if it's worth the trouble? Well, maybe once in a while....

During a recent off-season trip to the beach, I was not at all sure that the sunrise service was going to be worth the trouble. Getting up very early during vacation is not often my suggestion. Besides, I had only seen a brief announcement in the paper and had no idea what to expect.

It's cold on the beach at five o'clock on an April morning. Three or four hundred people have gathered, coming from all directions in the darkness. I'm shivering in my hooded jogging suit and belted raincoat. Gathered in a circle in the sand, together we sing "Christ the Lord Is Risen Today." The sky grows lighter. Someone sings "I've Just Seen Jesus," and the chills down my spine have nothing to do with the weather. At that moment, I think, no one would be the least bit surprised to see a bearded figure in robe and sandals come walking toward us along the edge of the sea.

Midway through the minister's message, he suddenly stops speaking. "I think we should all turn around," he says. The sun is rising, changing the placid ocean from gray to gold. After a moment of silence, we begin to sing "Amazing Grace." On the last verse, just as we reach the phrase, "bright, shining as the sun," the sun clears the horizon and fills the sky with the glory of Easter dawn.

Honestly. It happened just like that.

# twenty-four

## Do You Smell What I Smell?

Smell, they tell us, is the most evocative of all senses. (No, I don't know who "they" are, but I read it somewhere. Trust me.) It seems that psychological research has determined that smell, more than any other sense, triggers memories and emotions. Also growing in popularity is something called "aromatherapy," which I know nothing at all about. I always thought that's what people were doing when they rubbed a dog's nose in his "job" done in a socially unacceptable location. Or what a person with allergies might require in case of overdosing on potpourri in a Victorian gift shop.

I heard on the early morning news that a doctor has developed a new weight-loss program based on smell. Not yet being "clothed and in my right mind," at that hour of the morning, I'm not sure I got all the details, but the premise is that severely overweight people who inhale food-scented extracts such as banana or green apple just before a meal eat much less than they normally would. In some circuitous fashion, this olfactory deception sends messages to the hypothalamus, which fools the brain, which convinces the stomach that it's already had its dinner. And who says it's not nice to fool Mother Nature?

A recent study by the dental school of a major university has reported that root canal patients experience much less anxiety if the dentist's waiting room has been sprayed with a floral fragrance. Apparently it has to be flowers. Spice doesn't work. I wonder if the same thing would work in a labor room.

Studies also indicate that your house can be quickly sold—should you desire to do so, of course—if you either boil some cinnamon sticks in a pot on the stove or roast an onion in the oven while prospective buyers are poking their noses into the plumbing and kicking the banisters. The trouble is, there's no way to know which scent might make them sick and which would clinch the sale. I guess you could try both, but I doubt that the resulting odor would help the real estate agent win Salesperson of the Month.

I'm interested in all these new scientific smell-related breakthroughs because I am by nature a sniffer. If you sniff fruit before you buy it and meat before you cook it, you know what I mean. My son accuses me of being paranoid about sniffing around for natural gas, wood smoke, and overheated electric appliances. But listen, if you had to stand by and watch your house almost go up in flames because two under-intelligent delivery men jerked your old stove loose from its life support lines without turning off the gas or even extinguishing the pilot lights, wouldn't you be a bit sensitive to the smell of smoke? I'll take my bonfires out in the open field, thank you. It would save the local volunteer fire department a lot of trouble.

Smell is like an olfactory time machine. Catch one whiff of ditto fluid, and you're right back in first grade with all those fascinating purple-printed homework papers, reeking sharply and still slightly damp. If that doesn't do it, just remember those jars of white library paste that smelled good enough to eat—and some kid usually did. Gingerbread might put you right back in Grandma's kitchen. It was chilly this morning, so I pulled on the shirt closest at hand—my purple gauze beach cover-up that had just come out of the dryer. Clinging to it was the faintly coconut scent of suntan lotion. One sniff and I was back at the shore. I wish.

Would you believe the aroma of Tide has the same effect? It's been years since my friend Vicki and I spent a memorable and interminable afternoon washing and drying seven days' worth of laundry for twenty members of a youth mission trip to Arizona. No one had anticipated this particular problem, and by the time we found the solution the back of my Jeep Wagoneer was packed to the roof with dirty clothes. We never sat down for the hours it took to dry, fold, sort, and decide what to tell the girls whose underwear we melted in the dryer—the one we had been told to use because "it doesn't get as hot as the others." All we could say to one poor girl was, "Would you care for a waffle?" That's what her nylon slip came out looking like after it glued itself to the inside of the dryer. Oh, yes, The Silver Dollar Laundromat is firmly etched in my memory, and to this day, the smell of Tide takes me right back to the reservation.

Some of the olfactory impressions that stay with us are not so pleasant. I know that. However, I would just as soon not remember the day we almost had to evacuate the high school until the custodians found the offending and very dead groundhog stashed in a locker. Or the way my car smelled after an unfortunate encounter with a small black mammal with a white stripe down its back. Of course, that was nothing compared with our friends whose dog went three rounds with a skunk out in the woods and then slipped in the back door and made several complete circles through the downstairs before he was finally herded outdoors, leaving an eye-watering, breath-taking vapor trail behind him.

That's enough of that. I'd rather think about my favorite good-smelling things like...

   pine needles
   a just-bathed-and-powdered baby
   fresh-cut grass
   fat summer raindrops on a hot sidewalk
   warm honeysuckle nights
   cinnamon—in anything

And others that are nearing extinction like...

   sheets dried on the line on hot breezy day
   school rooms with oiled wood floors

bacon frying—outdoors—on a cool morning
a barn full of freshly mowed hay
citronella candles
freshly ironed, starched summer dresses
burning leaves on a brisk fall evening

Did you know that God also likes things that smell good? According to the Bible, the prayers of faithful believers rise to heaven like incense, their aroma pleasing to him. Disobedience, on the other hand, produces an offensive odor—a stench to the nostrils of God.

It's not hard to decide which is preferable, is it? Who wants to be a stinker?

# part five

# Insights and Outlooks

"Teach me what I cannot see..." **Job 34:32**

"Live and learn" is one of the few proverbs that doesn't seem to have another equally famous saying that contradicts it. We say, "Too many cooks spoil the broth," but "Many hands make light work." "He who hesitates is lost," but remember that "Haste makes waste." Views on living and learning tend to produce more consensus. My mother used to refer frequently to being educated in the "school of hard knocks," where, obviously, "experience is the best teacher." Most of us are gifted with more hindsight than foresight; we're more nearsighted than clearsighted. What we need is *insight*. Understanding. Jesus often spoke of people who had eyes but couldn't see—because they chose not to. Seeing may take a lot of living and learning. Things may look fuzzy for a while, as they did for the man born blind, who at first saw men looking like trees walking around. But sooner or later, we "see." These final chapters are reflections on some of my own personal eye-openers.

# twenty-five

## Roses, Flat Tires, and Great Expectations

Pride, the Good Book says, goes before a fall. In my case, it went before a flat. Actually, four flats. All on the same car. At the same time.

"A dream come true" isn't a term I use very often, but that's pretty much what my first teaching job turned out to be. That was back in the "olden days," when opportunities were so plentiful that many college grads got a teaching certificate as a type of job insurance: "You can always teach." Meaning, of course, if nothing more promising or profitable came down the pike. That had never been my attitude. As far back as I can remember, no matter how many times people said, "What do you want to be when you grow up?" I always said "a teacher." I was fortunate enough to walk right out of college into an ideal position: high school English, grades nine through eleven, and speech/drama sponsor. It was exactly what I wanted. I hit it off well with most of my students—well enough to be the target of mildly resentful jealousy-inspired comments about "you sweet young things" from a gray-haired veteran who must have been sticking it out until retirement.

It was spring, and we had just successfully presented our first dramatic performance—a class play. The stage was in the gym, which made rehearsals something of a challenge when the basketball team was practicing. But we had worked long and hard after school every weeknight except Wednesday, which was prayer meeting night for most of the area churches. The school and the local ministers had an understanding: the preachers would take turns praying at sports events and the school would schedule no Wednesday evening activities. That doesn't have a single thing to do with the story I'm telling, but isn't it interesting to see how much things have changed? Wouldn't the Supreme Court have a heyday if they got wind of that sort of collusion? Forget teaching. You'd have a new career—making license plates.

Anyway, I was having a wonderful time that night in spite of opening-night jitters, and so were the students. I'm not so sure about the audience, but they were kind. After the final curtain, the cast took their bows and then called me onstage. The leading man ceremoniously presented me with a dozen long-stemmed, red roses. Since I happened to be wearing a white wool sheath dress, the effect was, I thought, rather nice. The audience clapped, the cast and crew applauded, and I felt a little bit like Miss America.

After all the hugs and congratulations were over, makeup removed and costumes discarded, it was time to leave for the cast party. The darkened building was almost deserted when my husband and I sauntered out to my little maroon Corvair Monza with black bucket seats and four on the floor. At the moment, it was riding rather low on four—count 'em—*four* flat tires. Not slashed or anything—just deflated. Like my ego. Since this is not the sort of thing that happens by accident, it was clear that I had been the target of what was considered at that time serious vandalism.

I wilted a lot faster than those red roses did. Those tires weren't any flatter than my injured pride.

When we finally got to the party, the students were indignant, but I couldn't help wondering—was it one of them? Was there a Judas in the crowd? As it turned out, the culprit was a student I didn't know very well who was disgruntled about his grade. After being appropriately punished, he apologized, his sister apologized, his mother apologized. Everything was cool.

Dorothy's great expectations in Oz weren't any more shattered by the truth about the Wizard than mine were by the tire incident. I began my career thinking that if a teacher knew her stuff and conscientiously tried to be friendly, firm, and fair, everybody would respond in kind. I couldn't imagine that my love of literature wouldn't be shared by the youth of America. I was sure I could turn my students into creative writers and thinkers. I also thought that I could teach anybody the parts of speech! (Stop snickering.)

Obviously, I had led a very sheltered life.

Whatever I was able to teach my students that first year, they taught me more. Actually, most of what I believed proved true. But here's the big HOWEVER. No matter how hard you try, how sincere your intentions, or how well things seem to be going, not everybody is going to like, understand, and/or appreciate you. Somebody may even try to take you down. None of this, of course, would ever happen in the church. Right. (If you believe that, your yellow brick road is going to end in a *really* big surprise!)

Why let one negative experience overshadow all the positive ones? I don't know, but that's the way it is. Instead of accentuating the positive, we zero in on the negative. A mistake, a hurt, a failure, a misunderstanding—it's like a hangnail. Nineteen nails in perfect condition, but all our attention is focused on the one that hurts.

A harsh word used to reduce me to tears, criticism swamped me in self-pity. Through the years my expectations have altered, my hide has grown thicker, and now criticism affects me about like a BB on an elephant's behind.

Math is definitely not my field, but the way I figure it, I ended up with four roses for every flat tire. Four-to-one isn't a bad ratio. Any presidential candidate would call a vote like that a landslide. It wouldn't be a bad payoff in a horse race. Translated into grades, it would be about 80%—a respectable measure of success in pre-grade-inflation days. Look at it in baseball terms: four hits and a miss and you're batting .800! How's that for an all-star performance? Not too shabby.

I directed our church's district summer camp for girls grades two through six for nine years. More things went wrong the first year than during the other eight combined. It was the camp from you-know-where. During that one-week period, Murphy's Law came to life in every possible variation. I had worked very hard and was sure I had refined the registration process so to make it as slick as a hot buttered sliding board. I would have had those kids in and out of there in no time, except for the unexpected.

Perverse parents argued about room assignments. Walk-in registrations were at an all-time high. Groups of three and four refused to be separated, when no room had more than two available beds. Counselors didn't show up. All week, disaster followed disaster. The electricity went off in the kitchen, scheduled performers canceled out. Staff members brought their petty quarrels to me, like I was King Solomon or somebody. I couldn't go five minutes without answering a question or making a decision. It rained. Kids got sick. Kids got hurt. A girl very nearly drowned. I was on a first-name basis with the ER folks at the local hospital. And to top it off, there was a full-scale, all-out, run-rampant epidemic of homesickness.

The problem was, I didn't believe in homesickness. I truly thought there wasn't any such thing. Our strict ET-don't-call-home policy was being violated right and left by frustrated counselors who couldn't cope.

Every shred of compassion I showed toward the sniffling, sobbing little campers was faked. One of the older girls was a special trial. She exhausted my patience, my persuasive powers, and the telephone budget. All week I cajoled, coaxed, talked to parents, reassured. Actually, I think I was afraid that if one kid left, there would be a major exodus and dormitories would empty.

Did you ever, as a kid, shut your eyes and try to imagine how long eternity was? Well, in that one interminable week, I had a foretaste of eternity. I would lie awake in the wee hours, waiting for the next shoe to fall—or be thrown in my face.

Mercifully, we survived. Only one camper went home. On the last day, with the thousand details of closing camp and organizing the awards ceremony, I got a message. Holly

Homesick's parents wanted to see me.

I groaned. Oh, no. Here it comes. I gritted my teeth and went to face the music, expecting to be told how unhappy their little darling had been, how cruel I was, and what a failure the whole experience had been.

They were smiling. And they were holding out a gift-wrapped box. "We just wanted to thank you," they said, "for your patience. We know it's been difficult for you, and we really appreciate all you have done in encouraging our daughter to stay."

Dumbfounded, I accepted the gift with as much grace as I could muster. I opened the box. Inside was a handsome ceramic teapot. I am a tea-sipper from way back. Never touch coffee. They couldn't have known that, but they brought me a teapot! That teapot sits in my kitchen today, a heartwarming reminder that sometimes our greatest frustrations bring our greatest rewards.

When we're floating along on pink clouds of approval, it's wise to remember than sooner or later a dark cloud just may come drifting by as well. On the other hand, just when we're bracing ourselves for an unpleasant confrontation, we are handed an unexpected reward. So much for expectations.

In the well-loved story "The Gift of the Magi," O. Henry says that life consists of "smiles, sobs, and sniffles, with sniffles predominating." I'm not sure about the actual sniffle-to-sob or sniffle-to-smile ratios. I would prefer to think that smiles predominate, but between the frequent smiles and the infrequent sobs, there is quite a bit of sniffle-time. We can't expect life to be red-roses-in-a-long-white-box rewarding all the time. On the other hand, it's not healthy to sit around like Dickens' Mrs. Gummidge, whose constant refrain was, "I'm a lone, lorn, creetur and everything goes contrairy with me."

Sometimes even God doesn't meet our expectations. We get confused when bad things happen to good people. Especially when the "good people" are ourselves. That's what the bumper-sticker, TV-evangelist, health-and-wealth sound bite, megachurch-country-club, name-it-and-claim-it sort of pseudo-theology that has dominated the last couple of decades will do for you.

Disappointment fills the gap between expectation and reality. Unrealistic expectations = disappointment.

Think about this:

Did you ever hear a nurse complain about all the sick people she has to deal with? No sympathy there, right? What did the woman expect?

What kind of teacher would announce that school would be a nice place to work if it weren't for all those *kids* running around.

A new mother had better realize that babies cry. A lot. At inconvenient times. They also produce an incredible amount of more than mildly unpleasant laundry.

Save yourself a lot of unnecessary frustration. Don't harbor far-out expectations such as:

- More than one member of a family can learn to operate a dirty clothes hamper
- Children can learn the art of correctly loading a dishwasher
- Anyone other than a woman can install a new roll of toilet paper
- Males are capable of locating socks even when they are clean, folded, and in the right drawer

Never ask:

- How can a kid master the intricacies of Nintendo and not the operation of a washing machine?
- How can Game Boy whiz kids with quicksilver thumbs be totally incapable of turning off an ordinary light switch?

In other words, GET REAL. If we "get real" in our expectations about the Christian life (and the only way to do that is to get the big picture that the Bible presents rather than comfortable little sound bites), we will not let ourselves in for the kind of disappointment that can shake or even destroy our faith. That's the only answer I have for people who say, "It's not what I expected," "It didn't work for me," or even "God hasn't been fair."

If you believe any of the following, you are in line for a reality check:

- God will give me anything I ask for in faith.
- Christian service is unfailingly rewarding and fulfilling.
- Christian friends won't let you down.
- The church will provide the answer to all my social, emotional, and spiritual needs.
- Giving will always result in getting.
- My kids will turn out the way I planned.
- I won't get lonely, depressed, hurt, frustrated, fat, gray, or wrinkled.

This little poem, so old it may be new to many, is a beautiful reminder of what "get real" faith is all about.

### *"What God Has Promised"*

> God has not promised skies always blue,
> Flower-strewn pathways all our lives through;
> God hath not promised sun without rain,
> Joy without sorrow, peace without pain.
>
> God has not promised we shall not know
> Toil and temptations, trouble and woe;
> He has not told us we shall not bear
> Many a burden, many a care.

God has not promised smooth roads and wide,
Swift, east travel, needing no guide;
Never a mountain, rocky and steep,
Never a river, turbid and deep.

But God has promised strength for the day,
Rest for the labor, light for the way,
Grace for the trials, help from above,
Unfailing sympathy, undying love.

**Annie Johnson Flint**

I know that. So do you. But we're only human, and sometimes we forget. It's good to be reminded. I'm especially grateful for the "unfailing sympathy" part, because we don't always get that—even from those we love.

I came home from school the other day in a foul humor, almost at the point of tears from fatigue and frustration. It was budget time, semester grade time, and deadline time; besides that I'd just had a root canal, my back was acting up, and I had a headache. To top it off, people had been in my face all day with all kinds of requests, demands, and questions, questions, questions. I came in the door grousing and complaining.

My son Greg was the only sounding board available, so I sounded off, concluding with, "I don't want anyone ever to ask me another question!"

"But Mom," he pointed out with calm logic. "You're a *teacher!*"

Of course. What did I expect?

# twenty-six

## Little Things Mean a Lot

Pardon my cliché. In writing, one should avoid clichés like the plague. See? It's almost impossible.

So what's wrong with clichés? Nothing, except most of them are older than the hills. I know, I know. I'm doing it again.

Clichés may be overworked and worn-out expressions, but they are also true. That's how they got to be clichés. "Little things mean a lot" is true, so why look for a better way to say it?

Honestly, now, which bothers you the most: the fate of nations or the state of your house? the nation's fragile economy or your precarious bank account? crime in the cities or squabbling at the dinner table? Sure, the world is in a mess, but when was the last time you sat down and had a good cry over tension in the Middle East?

Take this quiz:

1. *I worry more about:*
    (a) the expanding national debt
    (b) my expanding waistline

2. *I am more upset over:*
    (a) the cost of putting a man on Mars
    (b) the cost of getting through the checkout at Kroger's

Things can get so big they don't mean anything. Like fourteen trillion dollars. Who can tell you how much that is? My puny little brain can't wrap itself around anything that enormous. It's just numbers. But I'll spend two hours looking for a two-cent error in balancing my bank statement.

"Do you remember what you said to me at church camp?" one of the teens asked me at church one day. It had been several years since she had been at the girls' camp I directed. I did a quick memory search and came up totally blank and rather embarrassed. I had to confess that I didn't recall. "You told me about fact, faith, and feeling," she said. "I've thought about that a lot and it's really helped me." An incident that didn't stand out in my memory among the many kids I had counseled over the years had been very important to her. Taking time to tell me about it was probably a "little thing" for her, but it meant a lot to me.

Willa Cather wrote of the Nebraska prairie where great distances were unimportant and "trifles dearer than heart's blood." For good or ill, little things do mean an awful lot. With that in mind, I have compiled...

## A RANDOM LIST OF VARIOUS AND SUNDRY BIG-LITTLE THINGS

a pencil-scrawled "I love you" note from a child
a pencil-scrawled "I love you" note from an adult
a moth hole in your softest, most-favorite sweater
hugs
bugs
a "thank you" letter from someone you helped a long time ago
a clean shirt that someone else ironed for you
Friday-night supper at a friend's house
a thumbtack sticking up through the sole of your shoe
an itch you can't reach
crocuses in the snow
a speck on your contact lens
an unkind word
a kind word
a blank tile in a Scrabble game (especially if you have a "Q")
a smile

a frown
a sprinkle of salt
a spoonful of sugar
an icy patch on the front steps
a splinter in your toe
a hummingbird

  Solomon warned us of the "little foxes that spoil the vines." It could hardly escape your notice if there were camels or donkeys out stamping around in your vineyard, but those pesky little foxes could sneak in right under your nose and totally destroy your livelihood. Remember the old rhyme about the battle and ultimately the kingdom that was lost all "for the want of a [horseshoe] nail"?

  Folk wisdom has always said that if you take care of the little things, the big things will take care of themselves. Look closely at the beautiful landscapes of many Impressionist paintings, and you will see that they are made up of thousands of tiny dots. So it is with life. The "big picture" is made up of lots of really important little things.

  Little things do mean a lot.

# twenty-seven

## Friendship 101
## or
## What I Didn't Learn in Kindergarten

"A friend is someone who is always there for you."

I sigh and reach for my red marker. "Vague," I scribble in the margin. "What does this *mean*? Be more specific."

*Give me a break, kid. Say something fresh and original. Spare me the same old sophomoric cliché.*

It's not easy finding a subject teenagers can write about with more enthusiasm than "How I Spent My Summer Vacation." I have found, however, that "friendship" ranks pretty high on the "I Suppose I Could Find Something to Say About It If You Absolutely Insist" list. At least I don't hear the word "stupid" muttered too often. Once they get the collective groan out of their systems and begin to write, the chances are pretty good that most of them will say, "A friend is someone who is always there for you."

This batch of papers was no different. But something was, because suddenly those overworked words started flashing in my mind like a neon sign on a cheap motel. I put the cap back on my red pen, took a sip of tea, and began to reflect on some lessons I had been learning about friendship while attending that most effective of all institutions of higher education: Experience U.

"When you go out into the world," says Robert Fulghum in his book *Everything I Need to Know I Learned in Kindergarten,* it's always a good idea to "hold hands and stick together." Friendship is holding hands and sticking together. That's about the best definition to come down the pike since

Charlie Brown said, "Happiness is a warm puppy." But one thing is for sure. The "holding hands" part is a whole lot easier than the "sticking together" part.

It's a chummy world we live in. Using a person's first name is no longer a symbol of intimacy. We're on a first-name basis with people we've just met and may never meet again. Receptionists who make appointments don't even seem to care whether you have a last name. Hugs have replaced handshakes as the greeting of choice. We like touchy-feely songs. We're willing to reach out and touch someone even if it takes three long distance companies or a $3.50 greeting card to do it. We're pretty good at holding hands.

Sticking together is another matter. That's what I learned about in Friendship 101.

LESSON NUMBER ONE: *Friendliness is not the same as friendship.*

Friendliness is highly prized in our society. Businesses spend a lot of money training their personnel to put their friendliest faces forward. Zealous telemarketers, with their unerring sense of timing, call at dinnertime and preface their sales spiel with carefully coached, warm-fuzzy greetings in the vain hope that we will think of them as old family friends. We expect friendly salesclerks and bank tellers and hairdressers. If the real estate agent or insurance representative isn't friendly, the deal is off. If hospitals and churches aren't friendly, we'll take our bodies and souls elsewhere. Even our computers have to be user-friendly.

As newcomers to a town where we knew no one several years ago, we were disappointed in the lack of friendliness in the church we attended. When the pastor came to call, he asked how we liked the church, so we told him. He must have passed the word along immediately, because the next Sunday I watched the organist at the close of the service as she charted a determined course in our direction. She breezed up, shook hands, introduced herself, assured us we were welcome, and sailed away, satisfied that she had done her Christian duty. She wasn't about to let anybody say *her* church wasn't friendly! And that was the end of that. She never spoke to us again. We weren't a bit sorry to "shake the dust off our feet" and move away a few months later.

A young woman I'll call Sherry was thrilled with the warm, friendly welcome she found at a church she began attending after taking a job and moving to a distant city. But after being nearly bowled over with friendliness, she was soon abandoned, lost in the single-on-Sunday syndrome, with virtually no opportunities for fellowship or service. No one seemed to notice if she happened to be absent—not even her Sunday school teacher, who worked in the same building as Sherry and never once said, "We missed you."

Friendliness is easy; friendship takes effort. Friendliness is casual; friendship takes commitment. Friendliness may be a passing encounter; friendship is a lasting relationship. It's good to be friendly; it's better to be a friend.

LESSON NUMBER TWO: *What you see is not always what you get.*

Somebody ought to design a true-false test for friendship. It ought to be easy to do in a test-happy society like ours. On second thought, I suppose there is one. It just takes a long time—maybe years—to administer, and you don't see the results until somebody flunks.

"False friend" sounds like an oxymoron (like "jumbo shrimp" or "tight slacks"), but it is an observable phenomenon. This enemy-in-friend's-clothing operates in a manner so subtle you can have a seemingly cordial encounter with her but then walk away wondering, "Did she really mean what I think she meant?" Freda (the False) is a master of the backhanded compliment: the I-don't-care-what-all-those-other-people-are-saying-about-you-I-think-you-are-a-nice-person sort of thing. Freda is sweet. She knows about honey catching more flies than vinegar. Flashing her brightest smile, she will get her own way at your expense and declare it was all done in your best interest. Maybe she believes it. But Freda was never your friend.

Fredas, thankfully, are scarce. Unfortunately, their natural habitat seems to be the church, where everybody wants to think the best of everybody else. I mention this only because it's an emotional and spiritual minefield, and when you see the symptoms you can be careful where you walk. And remember that the Lord understands. He had a "friend" named Judas.

LESSON NUMBER THREE: *Now you see her; now you don't.*

With a friend like Freda, who needs a friend like Phyllis? Nobody, but there she is: the fair-weather friend. This is the person who has been close to you, who sticks with you through everything—except anything requiring love, loyalty, courage, and commitment. When the going gets tough, the fair-weather friend gets going—in the opposite direction. Desertion can be worse than deception. Its no fun when your phone calls aren't returned, when promises are broken. But cheer up. Things can get better. Jesus also had a friend named Peter.

LESSON NUMBER FOUR: *A honest friend is a friend indeed.*

"What is so rare," asked the poet, "as a day in June?" With apologies to Mr. Lowell, I might ask, "What is so rare as an honest friend?" Now this is tricky ground, I know, but do not, I repeat, do NOT ask this friend for an opinion unless you want an honest answer. You won't have to guess what people are saying about you. You will know. Don't try to sweep problems under the rug—this friend hates dirt. The truth might hurt on occasion, but you are never in danger of backstabbing or betrayal. These friends, being so scarce, are quite valuable. Sometimes they are undervalued by those who don't know a diamond from a cubic zirconia. This is a serious mistake. If you have even one such friendship, you are fortunate. Take good care of it.

LESSON NUMBER FIVE: *(This is a math lesson. An equation.) Friendship = loyalty.*

There are no unknowns in this relationship. The loyal friend is the one who "sticketh closer than a brother." She stands up for you when others let you down. She knows that friendship is as much a verb as a noun; it's not something to talk about, but something to do. Loyalty speaks up when others remain silent. When others accuse, the loyal friend defends. She remembers when others forget. Friendship doesn't get better than this.

The Bible has a lot to say about friendship. It doesn't use the word "loyalty," which comes from an old French word meaning "allegiance," but it is very similar to the idea of "faithfulness" about which the Bible does have a lot to say. Barnabas (whose name means "Son of Encouragement") parted ways with Paul over young John Mark. Had this not happened, we might have come to know a lot more about Barnabas; but without his encouragement and loyal friendship, perhaps Mark's faith would have wavered, and the earliest of the Gospels to have been written would have been lost. Barnabas was also able to maintain his friendship with Paul in spite of their differences and was perhaps influential in restoring the broken fellowship between Paul and Mark.

The apostle Thomas has gotten bad press through the centuries, but no one could fault his courageous loyalty. He didn't try to ignore the danger that might be waiting if Jesus went to Bethany in response to the news of Lazarus' death. But that didn't matter to Thomas. "Let's go and die with him," he said. That's friendship.

"What are the most important qualities of a friend?" a Sunday school teacher asked recently. Loyalty and honesty were mentioned right away. "Anything else?" the teacher asked. My response was simply this: "If you have loyalty and honesty, you don't *need* anything else. If you have friends like that, count your blessings. If you are that kind of friend, you are a blessing."

It looks like I'd better toss away that red pen and admit that my students were right all the time. If Experience U. has taught me anything at all about friendship, it is this: *A friend is someone who is always there for you.*

# twenty-eight

## Are You Serving More... and Enjoying It Less?

I think this chapter title may have been inspired by an old cigarette commercial. If so, I apologize. But it just keeps running through my mind, and since there's not much up there to get in the way and slow it down, I need to get it out.

"Oh, my ears and whiskers, how late it is getting!" Whether you're a mom trying to get three kids and their assorted lunch bags, book bags, and gym bags out the door before the school bus driver whizzes right by your stop, or whether you're a working woman trying to beat rush hour traffic gridlock (how can it be *rush* hour at 10 mph?), or—quite likely—*both*, I just have one thing to say. Welcome to the White Rabbit Club. The only qualification for membership is the tendency to run around looking at your watch and wailing, "Oh dear, oh dear."

Whenever Alice encountered the White Rabbit during her adventures in Wonderland, he was always in a rush, scurrying around with all kinds of important things to do. Sound familiar?

Everybody who is busy is too busy. And every woman who is trying to do anything is trying to do everything. Each day is a whirl of nonstop activity. Listen, perpetual motion is a fantasy. (Except in the case of infants in utero during the last trimester of a pregnancy!) Physics is Greek to me, but I think the "perpetual" concept is that a motion will continue indefinitely without any input of energy. This, scientists have concluded, is impossible. We knew that. Even a two-year-old runs down for an hour or two each night.

Simple logic says no fuel, no fire. The kids at church used to sing, "Give me gas in my Ford, keep me chugging for the Lord." OK, it's not High Church stuff, but it gets the message across. Something has to keep us going. Otherwise, we get all used up. Tired. Sick. Sick and tired. Discouraged. Frustrated. Weary in well-doing. Color me burned out.

When it comes to crafts, my friend Diane is a world-class champion. Her creative and charming creations win national awards for the company she works for. But at Christmas, when most of us are knocking ourselves out to decorate our houses, she can hardly bring herself to put up a tree. When you start making decorations and trimming trees and tying bows in August, it's hard to muster a lot of enthusiasm for decking your own halls. And I certainly wouldn't want to answer for what might happen to anyone who stuck a red velvet bow in her face and yelled "boo!" on December 26.

This sort of burnout is temporary. We've all said, "Never again!" after directing the kids' Christmas pageant or chaperoning a teen retreat or organizing the annual mother-daughter banquet. After a while, we're revved up and ready to roll with new ideas and fresh enthusiasm. Some types of burnout, however, are a lot more serious.

In the movie *Teachers,* there was a character known to his colleagues and students alike as "Ditto." All he ever did was crank out stacks of dittoed worksheets for the students to fill out in class. Then he retreated behind his newspaper. One day Ditto died behind that paper. The bell rang. The students put their papers on the desk and filed out. The next class came in, picked up their day's work, and sat down to fill in the blanks. Ditto was still behind his newspaper. He was so burned out that when he checked out, nobody even noticed.

Young people can succumb to burnout, too. My sister-in-law Ruth (since she got her Ph.D. we call her "Dr. Ruth"), a public school gifted-education supervisor, told me about a revealing study of Presidential Scholars. These high school students with the highest GPAs, most academic honors, and most impressive extracurricular agendas are invited to Washington to meet the President each year and receive an award in recognition of their youthful accomplishments. It seems that a few years down the road, many of these brilliant young people do a total about-face. They end up doing anything *except* whatever it is they had studied and prepared to do. Such as being a professional surfer or running a goat farm in Wisconsin and making great cheese.

I don't know if the CDC in Atlanta has figures on this particular modern malady, but burnout occurs without regard for race, religion, family origin, age, gender—or occupation. It's strictly an equal opportunity problem.

But church work should be different, right? Well, maybe it ought to be, but it's not. The ministry has a high rate of burnout and drop-out. It's not just the high-profile televangelist who starts out doing good but ends up doing time, and not just the "perfect, people-person" pastor who cleans out the building fund and runs off to Acapulco with the church secretary. Many others start selling insurance or check themselves into rehab centers for shepherds who got clobbered with their own rod and staff or mowed down in a flock stampede.

Burnout hits the pew as well as the pulpit. It's just that not too many people notice until somebody says, "What happened to Beulah?" Nobody is sure why, but Beulah has hung up all her hats and is outta there. After forty years in the Kindergarten Department, one more chorus of "Deep and Wide" just might have put her off the deep end.

New Christians aren't immune. I've seen lots of them come in all fired up and before too long they exit stage left, all burned out. Old or new, it's a tragedy.

How can you keep from becoming one of these casualties?

Burnout is mostly in your head. I don't mean imaginary. I mean psychological, and that means it affects you in every way possible: emotionally, physically, spiritually. Severe cases, of course, need professional counseling, but the chronic, nagging, I-know-it-but-I-can-live-with-it type can benefit from a spiritual "wellness" program.

1. *Don't be pressured.* Not even when told, "There's nobody else." (I suppose at this point I should apologize to all those people I coerced in that manner.)
2. *Get help.* If it doesn't come through official channels, recruit your own. Look beyond the usual volunteers. At home, tap the endless energy and often hidden resources of your kids. I learned this from my sister, who has five. They cost you a lot of worry; they might as well save you some steps.
3. *Train someone to take over.* "Just until we find somebody else" could take until the Rapture. Train your own replacement. Then exit gracefully. And gratefully.
4. *Try a change.* Boredom is deadly. Do something different. Shock a few people. (You should see my high school students when I walk in dressed as Queen Elizabeth.)
5. *Take a break.* The church will survive. Your family will survive. The PTA will survive. The Kingdom of God will survive. You will survive. You may even revive.
6. *Plan.* Whether it's a menu or a musical production, think long-range. Even if you have to do it in the dentist's chair or in the bathtub or during the offertory.
7. *Prepare.* So obvious. So overlooked. It's the antidote to frustration.
8. *Be flexible.* Whatever won't bend will break. Always have Plan B handy.
9. *Learn to say no.* Not automatically, like you do when a kid says, "Mom, can I...?" but soberly, discreetly, and in the fear of God. Oops. How did that get in there?
10. *Enjoy.* This is probably the most important. Why? It "goes to motive," as they say on TV courtroom dramas. When our actions are motivated by love, no matter how difficult, they will bring us inner joy. If the joy is gone, it's time for a refueling, or burnout is inevitable. Why hasn't Mother Teresa burned out?

These are Ten Suggestions. Unlike a certain other Decalogue, they were not carved in stone by the finger of God. Feel free to take 'em or leave 'em. That's what I do.

# twenty-nine

## Lurching Along the Homeward Trail

"The Fight Is On" was one of my favorite "church songs" when I was a little girl. I don't know why, since I am (OK, used to be) basically a non-confrontational person. It was a great song which, incidentally, my mother and my sister used to like to play at wedding rehearsals before switching to "Here Comes the Bride."

Anyway, congregations used to sing with gusto rousing hymns like "Keep on the Firing Line" and "Sound the Battle Cry," which were bursting with the colorful military imagery that has always been a part of Christian tradition. Then a lot of people started getting bent out of shape about "militaristic" music and wanted to throw out everything that mentioned fighting or going to battle. If these well-intentioned folk encountered a bunch of Sunday school kids riding in the cavalry or shooting the artillery while belting out "I'm in the Lord's Army," they would have a collective coronary.

I can't seem to get worked up about this, although I do think kids are better off singing choruses with words they actually understand. I'm not sure a four-year-old knows what the cavalry is, not to mention the artillery. They do know "shoot" and the accompanying motions. Nevertheless, if you threw out all the references in the Bible—especially the Old Testament—to soldiers, armor, and warfare, you wouldn't have much left but the Song of Solomon. (*That's* an interesting book to teach the kiddies.)

The fact is, anybody who hasn't engaged the Enemy in battle somewhere along the line most likely hasn't gotten very far up the heavenly trail. The only problem I have with the military metaphor is the idea that once you've joined the army, you're constantly advancing at a steady pace, cutting a wide swath through all your problems like Sherman marching through Georgia. Well, you and I know it's not always Onward Christian Soldiers Marching to Zion Forward and Upward on the King's Highway. Maybe some stalwart souls march from earth to glory in a straight, unwavering line, but I think most of us get there by fits and starts. (Not too many fits, I hope!)

Running a race was one of St. Paul's favorite metaphors for the Christian life. This makes perfect sense in our fitness-fixated society, where people who apparently have no access to streets, sidewalks, or stairs actually go out and spend money on equipment on which they can run, walk, or climb.

Most of us are never going to win any kind of race unless it's to capture the remote control before a fanatical football fan makes it back from the bathroom, or be the first K-Mart shopper to grab the Blue Light Special. Of course, Paul makes it clear that the winner's crown is for anyone who finishes the race; you don't have to be first or even six hundred forty-seventh. Still, in our modern winning-is-everything society, the idea of racing might make us think we're in some sort of competition with each other. Now wouldn't it be terrible if *that* concept invaded the Christian community?

The Bible also calls the Christian life a "walk." Picture a toddler trying to get across a room: a few tentative steps, a few confident ones, and then he's flat on his Pampered behind with a surprised look on his face. Up again, off again, this time running full tilt—until he falls face forward. But every time he gets up, he's farther along than he was before. He will no doubt get distracted now and then. He may sit still for a while. He probably will shed some tears along the way and have to be picked up and set back on his feet from time to time. But he just keeps lurching along, and sooner or later he gets where he was going. Even after he grows up and gets really good at walking, he can still stub his toe or get tired out now and then.

One major toe-stubber is good, old-fashioned guilt. You're trained to feel guilty; blame it on your mother. Our childhood mealtimes were haunted by guilt over those starving children in India (or China or Africa) who shamed you for refusing to eat spinach. For me, it was pretty hard to see the connection. If I ate the slimy green stuff, it would certainly be of no use to anybody else. It would have made more sense to crate it up and send it off to the mission field like barrels of used clothing, but nobody ever suggested that. But whether I understood the connection or not, I felt the guilt.

When you grow up and learn to love spinach salad and spinach quiche and pasta with spinach, you still feel guilty. You're not a KGB spy or an axe murderer or a member of the Colombian drug cartel. You probably haven't defrauded any S&L stockholders or signed on with Heidi Fleiss or bribed a U.S. Congressman. You're certainly not wasting food that could help the starving children in Africa.

You can be prayed up and paid up and still feel guilty—not about things you do, but things you think you ought to be doing but aren't. Or even about things you *are* doing but think you ought to be doing more. Then a missionary comes to your church and talks about sacrifice. Ouch! There's nothing like the "s" word to make Jane Q. Christian squirm in her padded pew. You consider putting the house on the market and running right out to the Army-Navy store and picking up a pith helmet and a bottle of rhinoceros repellent. Instead, you pick out new wallpaper and re-do the powder room. Then you feel guilty that God hasn't given you an assignment involving mosquito netting and overgrown reptiles. And the guilt goes on....

Disappointments can also trip us up. Sometimes folks just don't shape up. The church lets us down. Things don't work out. We let ourselves be set up by some high-powered TV evangelist who calls himself a servant of God, lives like an Arabian oil sheik, and says, "When you pray for a new Cadillac, tell the Lord what color you want." If only we could stop treating God like some sort of celestial vending machine that dispenses favors when we drop in a quarter's worth of prayer, we might not be so let down when the health-wealth-prosperity-name-it-and-claim-it approach doesn't produce a phone call from Ed McMahon.

We like to figure out the answers to our problems and fill God in on the details: "Lord, You know," we say, and then proceed to inform him. Just in case God hasn't got it figured out, we offer instructions—or at least strong suggestions—on how he could go about achieving the desired results. Immediately. "Lord, give me patience, and give it to me RIGHT NOW."

Many people stumble over "unanswered prayer," not realizing that there really is no such thing. All prayers are answered, whether the answer is "yes," "no," or "wait." Sometimes it seems that our prayers are permanently "on hold." If you've never been frustrated like this, let me give you something to look forward to: you will be. You may even feel the way I did when I wrote this:

> I'll never forget the day
> I threw my devotional book
> Across the bedroom.
> "That's easy for you to say!"
> I exploded at the author.
> The topic was answered prayers
> And I was frustrated
> Because mine weren't.
> Or so I thought.
>
> You would think
> That after so many years
> Of being a Christian
> I would have known better.
> But then, I was in good company:
> David—
> "O my God, I cry out by day
> But you do not answer."

Jeremiah—
"Why is my pain unending?"
Isaiah—
"I have had enough, Lord."
And Job.

Job would have understood.
Through all the rejection
In his despair
He knew the secret
Before the Incarnation, before Calvary
Before the Resurrection, before Pentecost
Without the Church
Without the Bible
(Or even a devotional book)
He knew enough to say
"Though he slay me
Yet will I trust him."
And so will I, Job,
So will I.

No, I'll never forget that day—
And now I would be glad to tell you
About the urgent problem that caused me
To throw that book
Across the room.
Except
I can't even remember what it was!

"It came to pass," is maybe the most underappreciated verse in the Bible. Troubles *do* pass. The memory of pain fades away. If it didn't, every kid in the world would be an only child! If we just keep putting one foot in front of the other, sooner or later the path will level out and there will be smooth walking.

I did one of those open-the-Bible-and-put-your-finger-on-a-verse things the other morning, and this is what I found: "It will be named 'The Holy Highway.' God will *walk* there with you; even the most stupid cannot miss the way" (Is 35:8 LB).

That may not be the shortest verse in the Bible, or the longest verse, or the most profound, or the most poetic, but it certainly is the most reassuring. So we just keep lurching along that Highway—sometimes fast, sometimes slow, but always safe. And it is always an adventure.

# afterword

## 34 Steps to Writing an Article

One question that inevitably is asked of anyone who writes is "Where do you get your ideas?" Most writers say it's hard to answer that question, or they give some vague response about ideas coming from everywhere. Since people really seem to be interested, I decided to show exactly how to go about getting an idea and writing an article in a series of simple steps.

Here's how it works on a fine evening in early fall:

1. Turn on computer, access WordPerfect.
2. Stare at blue screen, blinking cursor.
3. Exit WordPerfect. (Save document? *What* document?)
4. Find yellow legal pad and favorite pen.
5. Pour glass of iced tea. Add lemon slice.
6. Pad barefoot onto deck, chase cat off glider.
7. Stare at yellow legal pad.
8. Observe wilting petunias. Resolve to water (as soon as article is written).
9. Watch son feed windfall pears to horses.
10. Wait for idea.
11. Watch yellow kitten sharpen claws on Rose of Sharon tree.
12. Watch gray kitten scratch higher, outdoing yellow kitten.
13. Stare at yellow legal pad.
14. Move wheelbarrow for son (on riding mower).
15. Watch horses slowly munch, drooling pear juice.
16. Wait for idea.

17. Sweep grass clippings from walk.
18. Take pity on petunias.
19. Return to glider.
20. Wait for idea.
21. Close eyes, savor evening breeze.
22. Watch Mama Cat stretch and yawn. Do likewise.
23. Snip pink rose.
24. Sit. Glide. Sniff rose.
25. Make squiggly lines on yellow legal pad.
26. Draw daisies on yellow legal pad.
27. Observe bird on fence. Get binoculars.
28. Watch weathervane gently revolve.
29. Wait for idea.
30. Twilight. See white barn turn from lavender to purple.
31. Listen to crickets commence their evening chorus.
32. Glance at legal pad. It's full!

See? Writing is easy. A piece of cake. Cake? Leftover carrot cake with cream cheese frosting?
Now *there's* an idea!